Tattwa Shuddhi

WORLD YOGA CONVENTION 2013
GANGA DARSHAN, MUNGER, BIHAR, INDIA
23rd–27th October 2013

1963–2013
GOLDEN JUBILEE

Tattwa Shuddhi

The Tantric Practice of Inner Purification

Swami Satyasangananda

Under the Guidance of
Swami Satyananda Saraswati

Yoga Publications Trust, Munger, Bihar, India

Printed by Bihar School of Yoga
    First edition 1984
    Reprinted 1992

Printed by Yoga Publications Trust
    Reprinted 2000, 2003, 2005, 2007, 2013

ISBN: 978-81-85787-37-4

Publisher and distributor: Yoga Publications Trust, Ganga Darshan, Munger, Bihar, India.

Website: www.biharyoga.net
        www.rikhiapeeth.net

Printed at Thomson Press (India) Limited, New Delhi, 110001

Dedication

In humility we offer this dedication to
Swami Sivananda Saraswati, who initiated
Swami Satyananda Saraswati into the secrets of yoga.

Contents

Salutations to Shakti

सर्वमंगलमांगल्ये शिवे सर्वार्थसाधिके।
शरण्ये त्र्यम्बके गौरि नारायणि नमोऽस्तु ते॥

O Shive,
You are the auspiciousness
Of all auspicious things,
And the fulfiller of all purposes.
You are the refuge,
O Trayambake,
O Gauri.
Unto you, O Narayani,
My salutations.

Introduction

Today yoga is practised in almost every corner of the world, but we do not really see any transformation in the consciousness of mankind. Where then does the fault lie? Is it in the practice itself? Not likely, because we can cite numerous examples of cases where it has been successful. It is more likely that the fault lies in the way we practise our sadhana; 'a bit of this and a bit of that,' whenever we care to do it. In order to eliminate this lop-sided approach to yoga, we will have to pay greater attention to the philosophy and practices of tantra, which is the source of yoga.

There is no use in just having a bird's eye view of a subject as vast as tantra, which has viewed existence from every angle or point of view. Through this 'in depth' study of the pattern of creation, its manifestation, its cause and effect in relation to the individual, the tantrics discovered the missing link which unifies the individual and the cosmos.

Once they had realized the way to bridge the gap, the tantrics devised methods and practices to guide others. Although these methods are inconceivably ancient, they have withstood the test of time, for the base on which they were developed, emphasized the necessity of inner experience for the evolution of an individual; not limited knowledge, but living breathing experience.

These methods of tantra are very systematic and precise. The practices are linked in such a way that the goal of

1

samadhi does not seem like a remote possibility, but a reality you can achieve here and now if you desire. The desire for samadhi is essential, for without the burning desire you can never get there. This desire should completely overwhelm and absorb you so that no other thought exists or dissipates the concentrated energy forces of the mind. Samadhi, tantra says, can be attained if only you care to look within instead of without. However, in order to develop the art of looking within, you have to follow the practices that have been specifically designed by tantra for this purpose.

Therefore, tantra lays greater emphasis on practice, rather than the philosophy behind it. Many accomplished tantrics are not even aware of the high-sounding philosophies extolled in the various translations or commentaries on tantra, because they are not impressed or captured by mere philosophy but by the transformation of the consciousness through its exposure to every level of experience.

Therefore, in order to understand tantra, you will have to delve deep into the practices and not merely attempt to understand it by bits and pieces of second-hand information. Try it for yourself and then pass judgement on tantra.

In order to do that, you will have to follow the procedures designed by tantra from beginning to end. There is little you can achieve by jumping into a lake if you don't know how to swim. Similarly, it is advised that sadhana should not be chosen on the basis of personal desires, but on that of personal growth and evolution, so that there is no danger of drowning.

For example, vama marga, kundalini yoga and so on may sound appealing and exciting, but unless there is a strong foundation, your sadhana is sure to dissipate. Tantra terms this foundation for all sadhana as *shuddhi* or purification.

However, on this point tantra differed from other philos- ophies, for what other philosophies termed as sin, tantra termed as a necessary experience for growth. Tantra says to utilize these forces of passion, anger, jealousy, guilt, shame and hatred by uniting them with their opposites. Only then can you experience unity. If you misuse these forces by creating a separation from their opposites, then the gap grows wider and unity becomes impossible. So, tantra speaks of purification but in a different sense. By the term purification it implies the release of energy from matter, so that the energy can unite with consciousness.

In order to achieve this aim of purification, tantra employed several methods, ranging from the gross to subtle and causal levels of purification. Tattwa shuddhi, which is included amongst these practices, stands out due to its effectiveness of purification at not just one, but all levels. It has emerged as one of the most important sadhanas which a disciple has to undergo on his journey from the outer to the inner world.

Without this purificatory process through tattwa shuddhi, the higher esoteric practices lead to darkness and despair. It is a very simple matter to understand. Vama marga, kaula marga, smashan sadhana, shyama sadhana or kundalini yoga require a very deep level of concentration which is only attainable when the mind has transcended matter and vibrates at the subtle frequency of pure energy. You have to be so proficient at attaining this state that it should happen as easily as at the press of a button. Only then can you hope to overpower the inner explosions that arise as a consequence of the practices. Otherwise you will simply remain at the level of material awareness, or else, if you transcend matter while still operating through the gross mind, the resulting experiences are likely to create a severe error in the personality.

It is not only from the point of view of sadhana that this purification has to take place, but even from that of living together in a harmonious society. The 'worries of the world' are assailing the human mind and the individual cannot cope with these traumas. Today man is at the height of mental tension, due to his inability to understand the mechanics of the mind.

If you ask the average person, "What is mind?", he will tell you that it is thought. He cannot even conceive that mind could be anything other than the psychological make-up. He does not know that, as you go deeper and deeper, you discover that hidden within these faculties is the potential power to create and destroy. Can you ever believe that the same mind which causes so much conflict in your life can create an entire universe; that the same ego which causes the pain and misery of attachment could explode the experience of oneness and unity; that dormant within you is the whole mystery of your life's journey from unity to diversity; that there exists in you a higher mind, which is the reflection of pure untainted consciousness? The sadhana of tattwa shuddhi enables the inner power of the mind to be revealed as a potential bridge through which the aspirant crawls from the transience of objective experience to the permanence of inner reality.

Essentially, tattwa shuddhi is a system designed to purify the whole of man's being. It begins with the gross form of purification and goes on to the subtle and psychic purification, culminating in the subtle awareness which prepares the aspirant for the experience of the energy and consciousness from which he has evolved. When one practices yoga over an extended period of time, it creates a mild awakening of *shakti* or energy, which can be felt in the psychic levels of the body and mind. However, tattwa shuddhi concentrates this awakening of energy and channels it by giving it a form, thus altering the basic awareness.

Tattwa shuddhi plays a primary role, not just in the context of practices related to mental, psychic and spiritual development, but even in those practices where the healing and curative processes are concerned. If tattwa shuddhi were practised before hatha yoga and the practices of yoga therapy, the result would be quicker and more enduring. Hatha yoga practitioners must understand that the body with which they are dealing is an aggregate and composite of five *tattwas* or elements, and hence tattwa shuddhi has a direct influence on the effects of the shatkarmas. *Shatkarmas* are also processes of purification of the body, but their influence is limited to the body's triple humours. Their effects do not stretch to the remoteness of the subtler layers, which can be achieved through tattwa shuddhi.

Tattwa shuddhi is the basis of all sadhana because it accomplishes the major spade work. Just as a farmer tills the land, fertilizes it properly, and then sows the seeds, similarly an aspirant first prepares the mind and body through tattwa shuddhi, then develops the richness of his inner experience.

1

Tantra

The aim of tantra is succinctly defined in the word itself. Tantra has been derived from the combination of two Sanskrit words: *tanoti* or expansion and *trayati* or liberation. This implies that *tantra* is the method to expand the mind and liberate the dormant potential energy. In order to understand tantra we have first to comprehend exactly what is meant by expansion of mind and liberation of energy.

The range of our experience related to the inner and outer world is usually severely limited. We can only see, hear, feel, taste and smell through the use of our physical senses. If one of our senses is impaired, our experience and knowledge related to that sense, is restricted and hampered. Therefore, perception and cognition are totally and mercilessly dependent on the senses. This is a limiting adjunct in our lives because knowledge derived through the senses is restricted by the boundaries of time, space and object.

Time, space and object exist only as categories of the individual mind. If there is no individual mind, there is no time or space or object, and vice versa. These three categories of mind are finite and cannot be regarded as the source of infinite or imperishable knowledge. As long as we function through the realm of the senses and mind, we cannot transgress these finite and restricting boundaries.

For example, to see the lustrous beauty of a flower, it is necessary to have the flower in front of your open eyes; to smell the fragrance of sandal or lavender, it is necessary to have it in close proximity to the nose; to taste the sweetness of chocolate or the pungency of chillies, they have to be eaten. This type of experience is called objective because it is dependent on the presence of an object, the senses, and the mind in relation to both of them.

However, there is a range of experience when you can see with your eyes closed, taste in the absence of food, hear the sound of music without any instrument to cause it. That is a purely subjective experience and it is unbound by the categories of finite mind. Knowledge gained through a subjective experience is far more accurate and precise than that gained through an objective experience, because it is the consequence of an expanded mind.

Expansion of mind is that phenomena which allows an individual to experience beyond the realm of the senses, time, space and matter. In that realm, you are unbound by distance and time. You can travel into the past or future and know the happenings at places where you are not physically present. This is known as expansion of mind but it is unattainable as long as you are bound by sensorial experience. Mind operating through the senses and ego categorizes all experiences according to *raga* and *dwesha* or likes and dislikes, which it has inculcated. This imposition of the mind creates a distortion of the knowledge received from any experience and does not allow for the growth of pure, refined knowledge.

Knowledge gained through an expanded mind, gradually evolves and finally culminates into intuitive knowledge, which has been declared as eternal, absolute and the true knowledge. But the expansion of mind does not happen overnight. One goes through a long range of experiences, some mild, some intense, some pleasant, some unpleasant. It is a gradual growth which finally culminates in absolute knowledge or *brahma jnana*.

A child does not grow into an adult overnight. The transformation is gradual. The line of demarcation between child and adult is so subtle that one can never point out where one ended and the other began. Similarly, man's consciousness is evolving all the time. Mind is expanding and crossing new boundaries. The transformation is taking place but the pace is gradual and the change subtle.

In order to accelerate the evolution of mind and direct your own transformation, you will have to turn to the practice of tantra and yoga. These practices are designed to accelerate the liberation of energy from matter and manifest the pure innate consciousness which is the source of all knowledge.

Aim of tantra

The mind which we use in day to day life for perception and cognition ordinarily acts through the senses. But if we can introvert the senses and turn the mind inwards, it manifests itself through inner experience and an expanded mind. Thus matter is separated from energy, thereby liberating the energy or *shakti* principle, which then unites with *shiva* or consciousness, creating homogeneous awareness.

Just as a river expanding into the ocean loses its limitations and restrictions, similarly the finite mind expands into the cosmic or infinite mind and thus becomes a receptor and transmitter of the truth. When this occurs, there is a resulting explosion of energy and the inherent consciousness is freed from the matter. This can be likened to the kundalini experience and this has always been the aim of tantra.

Other philosophies also reached out towards the same goal, although the paths may differ. In Vedanta philosophy, there is the concept of *Brahman* or the indivisible, homogeneous, all-pervading reality or consciousness. The word Brahman is derived from the root *brihan*, which means to expand, and can therefore be understood as expanding consciousness. It is this brahmic awareness, present in each one of us, which is responsible for the highest knowledge. It exists as one or the whole, towards which we are constantly striving to unite.

In tantra, this concept is interpreted as shiva or unconditioned consciousness, which exists as a silent witness

8

within each one of us. Whether it be the Brahman of Vedantins or purusha of Samkhya philosophy or Shiva of tantra, it is essentially the same concept. However, the difference between tantra and most other philosophies is that they lay many restrictions on the life of the aspirant and demand strict adherence to rules, whereas tantra allows scope for the development of each and every individual regardless of his stage of evolution. Tantra says that, whether you are a sensualist or a spiritualist, an atheist or theist, whether strong or weak, rich or poor, there is a path for you which you have to discover.

This is the goal of tantra, not occult sex, nor black magic, nor the acquisition of *siddhis* (psychic powers), nor licentious living. These have never been the aim of tantra. Tantra may have been misinterpreted by some in this manner, but that is a different matter altogether. Moreover, we can hardly rely on those who have failed to achieve homogeneous awareness to present a true analysis of tantra.

Tantra: a liberal path to liberate the mind

From time to time, the tantrics experimented with various methods and paths in order to achieve this aim. Their belief was that every man cannot tread the same path, because each person is poised at a different level of evolution. It is often said that, "One man's meat is another man's poison." The tantrics realized the necessity of including a spiritual path for each and every individual, whether he was a gross sensualist, profound philosopher, or an evolving yogi.

They often experimented with methods that would seem extremely gross and sensual to the average eye. These practices were considered bizarre for they involved meditating beside a naked woman, or near a dead body and many other tantalizing practices. Many opposed and criticized tantra for this reason and felt such methods were just an excuse for indulgence and in no way induced spiritual experience.

However, the inherent sincerity and steadfastness of the tantric proves otherwise. If he experiments with licentious sex, alcohol and drugs, it should not be the act which is judged, but his mental awareness, attitude and purpose for which he practises it. If he invokes spirits and performs rites and rituals which can be commonly referred to as 'black magic', we should not criticize him on the basis of his actions, but on the basis of his motives for doing so.

This is the essential difference between a tantric and an ordinary gross individual who may practise the same, but purely for sensual enjoyment and material gain. Through these practices a tantric systematically explodes the powerful and potential force of energy within him. Passion, fear, hatred, love, anger and so on are energy forces and he meets them face to face. If properly tamed, these energy forces can lead to many higher experiences. During meditation, if he is able to maintain his concentration, they appear in the form of visions, dreams, varying sounds, clear voices, different types of music and even objects, animals and human beings can be materialized.

The proof of a tantric's prowess lies in his ability to remain undeterred. He does not become overwhelmed by experience, nor is he ridden by fear. A man of infirm mental make-up, erratic emotions and distracted mind may suffer a psychic attack, nervous depression or even insanity, should he venture to do such or similar practices.

What are fears and passions but forces of energy? The emotions we experience in our daily lives are enough to drive a person crazy. Balance cannot be maintained and people are driven to insane acts of murder, rape and crime. What will happen if your mind is confronted by the full force of fear and passion that exists within you? Could you handle that? However, the tantric is able to explode the experience from within his unconscious; he is able to master this powerful internal force and convert it into a greater and subtler force which he himself can direct at will.

However, it was found that many of these practices resulted in 'mind blowing' experiences from the unexplored dimensions of mind, which the average individual was incapable of withstanding. So, the tantrics developed other practices which could lead the aspirant smoothly and mildly through graded experiences, within his capacity. Extreme practices were left aside for those who were strong and resolute in the face of powerful inner experiences. These milder techniques, which set the foundation for advanced practices, include hatha yoga, kriya yoga and japa, as well as tattwa shuddhi.

Tantric literature

Tantric literature clearly enumerates these and several other practices. However, tantric literature is extremely vast and often incomprehensible to most people because it is recorded in symbols, imagery, myth and allegory. This is with due reason, too, because the practices of tantra in the hands of one who has not overpowered his instinctive nature are like dynamite in the hands of a child.

Tantric sadhana ensures results within a very short period, which accrue as siddhis or psychic powers. But these siddhis are of little consequence for the evolution of consciousness. Rather, they often prove to be a barrier because many aspirants remain forever entangled by the benefits derived thereof. Therefore, in tantra, this knowledge is very wisely obscured from the layman in such a way that only the sincere aspirant can understand the meaning of the symbology.

In total, there are sixty-four tantras, i.e. texts on tantra, dealing with varied sciences, such as how to control one's mind and also the mind of another person, how to attain immortality, how to achieve virility and sexual prowess, and so on. The famed commentarian, Bhaskaraya, has included eight more texts into the list, making a total of seventy two tantras. Tantric science is so varied that there is a path for everyone. Even the person who is not at all 'spiritual' can find a way to expand his consciousness.

Along with the tantric texts, the Puranas also deal with the tantric sciences. The Puranas are mostly allegorical and many tantric practices have been disguised further in the

11

garb of mythology. They extol the lives and legends of *devas* and *rakshasas* (divine and demonic beings) and through their colourful stories, we are led to the path of tantra. It is in the *Srimad Devi Bhagavatam* and *Mahanirvana Tantra* that the practice of tattwa shuddhi has been divulged.

Worship of shakti

However, the student of tantra will discern one important fact at the outset: that although the science of tantra confesses to an all-pervading reality, it also pays homage to and maintains strict faith in the presence of the dual aspect of *shiva* (consciousness) and *shakti* (energy). Shiva is the static principle which exists as pure unconditioned consciousness, but it is only at the behest of shakti, the kinetic principle, that shiva, who otherwise remains inert, is motivated into action.

This is symbolized in the *Tandava Nritya* of Shiva, the dance of Shiva, after which he has been named Nataraja. For every aspect of shiva, there is a corresponding aspect of shakti. If shiva is Shambhu, then shakti is Shambhavi; if shiva is Maheshwara, shakti is Maheshwari; if shiva is Bhairava, shakti is Bhairavi; if shiva is Rudra, shakti is Raudri. Shiva and shakti are complementary at every level.

From this concept arose a sect known as *Shaktas*, i.e. followers of the philosophy of shakti, who consider shakti as the all-pervading reality. In fact, in the *Shakta Puranas*, the question arises whether the ultimate reality is male or female. Shaktas unanimously assert that the creator of the universe could only be a female, for creation is an inherent principle of the female and not the male. The worship of shakti reached its zenith only under the influence of tantra. Vedic theology was male orientated and the goddesses or shaktis received only peripheral roles. This is not so in tantra.

All tantric practices are designed to awaken the inherent shakti or energy, which is the female or negative principle. Without awakening this energy, consciousness can never manifest. This is the claim of tantra and today science is even verifying the tantric claim. According to modern physics, matter and energy are interconvertible. Tantra goes one step further and says matter, energy and consciousness are interconvertible. But matter cannot be transformed into pure consciousness without the medium of energy. Therefore, in tantra, shakti stands at par with shiva.

Manifestation of shiva/shakti in the body

It is the claim of tantra that these aspects of shakti and shiva (energy/consciousness) are not abstractions, but a tangible reality existing within the framework of the body/mind structure. Tantra states that shakti, which represents the subtlest manifestation of energy, lies coiled like a serpent at the root of the spine and is known as *kundalini*, whereas shiva or consciousness, is located in the region of *sahasrara chakra*, the highest evolutionary centre in man, which is situated at the crown of the head.

However, due to the grossness of the body/mind which is governed by sense experience, these two powers remain dormant in the majority of people. In order to awaken the latent force of kundalini, it is necessary to intensify the quantity and quality of *prana*, the vital energy force in the region where it is situated.

Once awakened, kundalini has to be directed upwards to unite with shiva or consciousness in the region of sahasrara. During her ascent the kundalini shakti passes six energy circuits or *chakras*, which are the storehouses of energy, and thus supercharges each chakra. These chakras are the junction points of *nadis* or energy channels and vibrate with varying frequencies, ranging from gross to subtle. Inherent within the chakras are dormant creative powers which partially manifest in daily life. Their full potential can only be awakened when kundalini shakti pierces through them on her journey to unite with shiva.

The basis of tantric sadhana

The essence of tantric sadhana can be classified into three stages of *upasana* or worship. The tantric believes that every act, however mundane, if offered to the higher force within oneself or abounding in the universe, becomes meaningful and a medium through which he can transform his awareness. These three stages of upasana are:

1. *Shuddhi* – purification of the gross, subtle and psychic elements or tattwas.
2. *Sthiti* – illumination resulting through concentration, which is achieved by refining or purifying the elements.
3. *Arpana* – unification with the higher force within oneself, or realization of the cosmic consciousness.

Thus shuddhi is the basis of all tantric sadhanas, whether they are based on *vamachara*, *kaulachara* or *vedachara* practices. These are the three major categories of tantric sadhana and they have all emphasized the requirement of shuddhi as an integral part of spiritual practice and evolution.

Tattwa shuddhi in the tantras

Tantrism has been marked as one of the most distinct and revolutionary facets of Indian philosophy, due to its amalgamation of so many heterogeneous elements. It is, therefore, no wonder that an aspirant in search of spiritual experience can easily delve into the tantric literature to find a suitable path. The practice of tattwa shuddhi has been derived from this wide source of tantric literature.

Tantric practices can be easily discerned from non-tantric practices by their intensive use of sacred formulae, symbolism and ritual orientated practices. External worship and ritual are considered essential in tantra to create a suitable environment for luring the higher and subtler forces. These rites are carefully selected to symbolize the inner forces which are unleashed through esoteric sadhana, and are often detailed processes lasting for several hours.

The practice of tattwa shuddhi described in this book has been taken from the ritual of tantric worship, which includes *nyasa* (consecration of the body), *prana prathishta* (installing life and power into the mandala), *panchopchara* (five ingredients offered in worship to the tattwas), and *japa* (mantra repetition), which are discussed later. Due to ample use of exoteric ritual, i.e. application of ash and fasting, and esoteric ritual in the form of visualization of yantra and mandala, it is easy to discern that tattwa shuddhi is derived from tantric sadhana.

References to tattwa shuddhi can be found in many of the tantras, as it is an essential part of all esoteric sadhanas. In the *Tattwa Sambara*, one of the sixty-four tantras, there is a description of how we can cause the elements to appear. *Mahanirvana Tantra* also enumerates this practice as a part of tantric upasana or worship. However, in the *Srimad Devi Bhagavatam*, a shakta Purana extolling the glories of Devi, this practice is given in full detail.

These, as well as other tantric texts, strongly assert that tattwa shuddhi is a necessary step towards higher experience, as it refines the basic elements from which spiritual experience unfolds. Today, we are becoming aware that matter is but an extension of consciousness, or an aspect that consciousness has assumed. Thus in order to experience the effulgence of consciousness devoid of matter, it is first of all necessary to refine that into which it has manifested. This process of refinement is triggered through tattwa shuddhi.

In order to transcend the experience of matter, it is imperative that the practice you employ should be based on a thorough knowledge of the principles related to the mind, body and consciousness. The consciousness is unable to transcend matter, due to the inherent laws governing the tattwas which compose the entire structure of your existence. Tattwa shuddhi is based on a very profound understanding of these principles and aims to restructure their grossness and density.

Tattwa shuddhi is a firm step towards the fulfilment of the goal set by tantric sadhana, which is to experience the light of energy and consciousness. It is not enough to merely state that all matter has evolved from consciousness. The truth cannot be realized by intellectual knowledge, nor verified by philosophical reasoning. It is only through one's practice

15

and personal experience that one can induce a capacity to understand any spiritual truth.

Personal experience, which is greatly emphasized in tantra, becomes possible through the practice of tattwa shuddhi. The rich imagery placed before the mind has been carefully selected to imply that everything which exists in nature is a part of energy and consciousness. The sadhaka is taught to realize that each part of his body is functioning through shakti, and by continual practice each tattwa is divinized, until it is seen, not as gross inert matter, but as a form of shakti which represents consciousness.

This energy, which is locked up in matter, is released and transformed through the practice of tattwa shuddhi. Energy vibrates in the body as a pranic flow and when this flow is increased it awakens a higher experience. Although several yogic practices are designed to increase the flow of prana, tattwa shuddhi allows for both increase and transformation of prana.

It is also important to understand that, through inner concentration on the tattwa yantras, we are not only heightening the level of prana, but also directly influencing the chakras. Each tattwa is intimately linked with a particular chakra and this in turn prepares the basis for awakening of kundalini and its ascent to sahasrara.

Tantric sadhana is given to an aspirant on the basis of his level of evolution. Thus there are three grades of sadhana, known as *sthoola* (exoteric), *sukshma* (subtle), and *para* (transcendental), one progressively culminating into the other. The different methods of pratyahara, such as asana, pranayama, mudra, bandha, as well as all forms of *pooja* or worship, can be categorized as sthoola sadhana. Sukshma sadhana, which develops as a consequence of perfection in the methods of sthoola sadhana, can be termed as a process of *dharana* (concentration) on a mantra or symbol or *ishta devata* (one's personal symbol). This gradually leads the aspirant to the stage of *dhyana* (meditation), which is considered to be para or highest sadhana, culminating in samadhi.

Tattwa shuddhi comes under the category of sukshma sadhana, thus providing the necessary link for the development of higher practices. It is within the capacity of anyone who has sincerely practised yoga for a few years. When an aspirant's body and mind are sufficiently prepared in the stages of pratyahara and the mind is easily introverted, then tattwa shuddhi develops concentration or dharana. Perfection in this practice induces spontaneous dhyana or meditation, which leads the aspirant to *tattwa jnana* or realization of the subtle essence behind the form.

2

Tattwa Shuddhi in Brief

For thousands of years, the yogis have stated that man's physical body extends far beyond what the eyes can perceive, that he is far more than just flesh, blood and bones and that, like all matter in the universe, he is a composition of many elements, both gross and subtle, which combine to constitute his body and mind.

Today science is validating this claim. With the advent of modern technology, science has travelled beyond the boundaries of physics into the realm of metaphysics. It now includes the possibility that the building blocks of matter are in fact composed of millions of electrons, neutrons and protons moving in particular patterns to form that which we call matter. This was known to the yogis who called them *anu* and *paramanu*.

If this is true, then we have to base our beliefs on the theory that the world of matter is non-existent, that what we perceive as tangible, real and whole, such as the walls of our house, a chair or a television, are in fact fields of highly charged particles of energy moving at different frequencies and levels of vibration, to compose matter. This is precisely what the yogis have been saying since ancient times.

This explains how a yogi, who is able to raise his psychic frequencies to that of the atoms and molecules reverberating within matter, can see through it. The matter does not exist as a barrier for him: he only recognizes the energy charged particles. Several experiments have been conducted in India where a *siddha* or perfect yogi is able to know what is happening in a room adjacent to his, without going there.

Science today has explored the nucleus of an atom, thus transforming matter into energy. Many thousands of years ago, the yogis exploded the nucleus of their being within the laboratory of the body and mind, thus asserting that human beings are composed of energy or prana. This energy vibrates at varying frequencies and later condenses to form the physical body.

The fact that science has transcended the realm of matter and discovered the energy behind the form is, no doubt, an important breakthrough. However, energy is not the final stage of manifestation. Beyond energy there is consciousness, which is responsible for everything that takes place in the universe. It is from consciousness that this physical body, as well as all matter, has evolved.

Although science has yet to fully grasp this idea and is only beginning to dwell on its possibility, there is a group of scientists who have begun to probe into the role of consciousness in every form of creation. They have stated that an experiment conducted in a laboratory by two people, under the same conditions, may not necessarily produce the same result, as the effect produced is influenced by the consciousness of the observer. Thus consciousness becomes the influencing factor and the experimenter can no longer be termed as an observer; rather he is a passive participant.

Therefore, objective analysis alone is incomplete, and all theories of matter and energy that we conjure up in the laboratories should not be considered final or absolute. The result is also dependent on the consciousness of the observer, whose faculties through which the consciousness is acting may not be sufficiently refined or tuned to higher frequencies, in which case it will interpret all information according to its own erroneous perception.

The yogis, on the other hand, through their continuous inner quest, discovered the relation and interchangeability between matter, energy and consciousness long ago. They have stated that consciousness manifests as energy, which condenses into matter. If we wish to experience this consciousness free from matter, we will have to reverse the process of evolution back to its original cause. This is achieved through purification, by eliminating the extraneous factors in the mind and body. It is here that tattwa shuddhi becomes effective as a sadhana.

Outline of the practice

Purification and transformation of the subtle elements composing the body and mind takes place through self-reflection and meditation. Tattwa shuddhi is a dynamic form of meditation and self-reflection. It is not a passive practice of meditation in which you have to concentrate for hours and hours on one symbol. Neither does it cater for the mind to become accustomed to images arising during the practice. On the contrary it demands abstract mental creativity to encourage spontaneous concentration by absorption of mind in the vast potential of rich imagery.

Through the practice of tattwa shuddhi, the inner awareness is readily immersed in creating *tattwa yantras* (geometrical diagrams of the elements), *Papa Purusha* (the sinful man) and the mandala of *prana shakti* (the form of creative energy). Although one has certain basic guidelines to follow, there is ample scope to create and utilize the enormous supply of inherent primordial imagery.

In the practice, you first create a mental and psychic awareness of the elements and their respective yantras in the body. You witness the process of one tattwa emerging from another and thus delve deeper and deeper into the subtler layers of existence. After discovering the universal or cosmic energy within, that force is used to dispel internal imbalances.

Approaching the problem of imbalance within yourself from a higher level of awareness makes it easier to harmonize those forces, as you are doing it through a mind that has become strong and powerful. After this transformation, you recreate the elements in the physical body in reverse order. The practice then culminates in a vision of prana shakti herself. It is prana acting through the tattwas, karmendriyas and jnanendriyas which allows knowledge and action to take place, and, therefore, obeisance is paid to prana.

The culmination of the practice is the application of *bhasma* or ashes. The significance of applying bhasma and the vision of prana shakti will be dealt with later. Nevertheless it should be known from the beginning that they should not be confused with one's religious views. Tattwa shuddhi is a practice of the tantric science and has nothing to do with religion.

The *Srimad Devi Bhagavatam Purana* and the Upanishads, both state clearly that *karma* and *dhyana* (action and meditation) lead one to *moksha* (liberation).They are like the two wings of a bird. Just as both wings enable it to fly off the ground, so karma and dhyana are necessary to take the awareness from a tamasic state to the higher state. In tattwa shuddhi, meditation is achieved by concentrating on the tattwa yantras and other visual forms created in the *chidakasha* (psychic space in front of the closed eyes). Karma is performed through the application of ash and fasting.

The basic beliefs of tantra are evident in the practice of tattwa shuddhi. Firstly, this practice is an *upasana* or a homage to the cosmic energy principle, prana shakti, which gave birth to your body and mind. Worship of shakti is considered to be an unavoidable part of tantric upasana because tantra believes that, without the power of shakti, not even a blade of grass can move. Moreover, the traditional practice of tattwa shuddhi entails both the external rituals which accompany an act of worship and the inner attitude of reverence towards a higher reality.

Secondly, the practice utilizes the basic tools of tantra: yantra, mandala and mantra, which are present in each and every facet of the tantras, from 'black magic' to vama marga to tantric music, art and architecture, or simply the practices of yoga. These instruments develop one-pointed concentration and are an essential part of tattwa shuddhi. Tattwa shuddhi can be used as an aid to meditation and advanced esoteric practices, or as a complete sadhana by itself. Although the purpose of the practice is purely spiritual, one can surely experience the benefits in all realms of existence.

Prerequisites of the practice

The person most qualified to practise tattwa shuddhi is one who has trained his body and mind to a sufficient degree through hatha yoga and ajapa japa. The aspirant is required to sit in a steady position, preferably siddhasana, siddha yoni asana or padmasana, for one hour, during which time his mind should not become distracted or externalized. This means that the aspirant should have a healthy body and mind before he begins the practice of tattwa shuddhi. The practice should not be undertaken by one who is suffering from physical ailments. It is better to wait until the illness is cured before beginning the practice.

Tattwa shuddhi is a system of dharana and it is necessary to introvert the mind before commencing the practice, so that the state of dharana is easily achieved. It is for this reason that the *Srimad Devi Bhagavatam Purana* suggests that the aspirant should induce *pratyahara* (sense withdrawal) through pranayama or trataka, prior to the practice of tattwa shuddhi.

Tattwa shuddhi sadhana requires a basic knowledge of the location of the chakras in the body, the ascending and descending passage of prana in sushumna, *ajapa japa* (mantra repetition), and other relevant yogic practices.

Apart from these prerequisites, the attitude or *bhava* of a sadhaka is an important factor in all tantric sadhana, because it is through the inner attitude that purification is enhanced. If your bhava or attitude is that of devotion, open-mindedness and acceptance, the effects of the practice are far greater. A closed mind can never experience unity. It is caught within the boundaries of bias and prejudice, which are an impediment to spiritual experience.

In tattwa shuddhi, it is necessary to overcome the nagging intellect and develop devotion, which is a consequence of inner faith and conviction. Without the bhava of devotion, spiritual sadhana dwindles into a mere act of ego and eventually destroys the elevating experience attained through the practice.

3

Tattwa Shuddhi:
Process of Purification

The word *tattwa* is broken up into two syllables: *tat* meaning 'that' and *twa* meaning 'ness'. Therefore, tattwa signifies 'thatness', which can be further understood as 'the essence which creates the feeling of existence'. Tattwa is also known as bhuta in the scriptures. *Bhuta* is another Sanskrit term which has a wide range of connotations, but as its meaning coincides in part with tattwa, the two words are used synonymously. The five elements are commonly referred to as *pancha mahabhuta* or *pancha tattwa*.

Shuddhi is the act of purifying and sadhana is the act of perfecting. Therefore, tattwa shuddhi or bhuta shuddhi sadhana can best be understood as 'perfecting purification of the essence which gives rise to the feeling of existence'. Thus it is a process by which we purify the subtle essence of tattwas of which the body is composed, as well as the underlying consciousness related to those elements.

The tantric tradition believes that the ultimate experience is preceded by many stages of purity. Not purity in a religious, moral or ethical sense, but as a scientific process created in the laboratory of the body and mind. The tantras talk about tattwa shuddhi or purification of the subtle elements: *prana shuddhi*, purification of the vital force elements; *chitta shuddhi*, purification of the psychological elements; *deva shuddhi*, purification of the divine elements; *atma shuddhi*, purification of the elements constituting the unconscious. Each of these

24

practices is related to the unleashing of energy and separation of consciousness from matter. Tantra asserts that it is only when this happens that true spiritual experience begins.

Just as a potter fires his works of art in a burning hot kiln, tattwa shuddhi prepares an aspirant for the tempestuous and stormy path encountered through the higher practices. Whether you practise vama marga, dakshina marga or kaula marga, hatha yoga, kriya yoga, kundalini yoga, raja yoga, or any yoga, you will have to incorporate tattwa shuddhi to give momentum to your progress in sadhana.

Meaning of purification

Through tattwa shuddhi sadhana, we purify the tattwas or the elements and also the senses and perceptions connected with them. The sense of hearing and auditory nerves are purified by repetition of mantra. The sense of sight and optic nerves are purified by witnessing the yantras and mandalas. The sense of touch and tactile nerves are purified by the application of bhasma through anga nyasa and kara nyasa. The sense of smell and olfactory nerves are purified by pranayama, and the sense of taste and gustatory nerves are purified by fasting or sattwic diet.

However, purification through tattwa shuddhi should not only be conceived as physical purity. Purification in that sense is only for those of little understanding. Tantra lays greater emphasis on purity at the gross, subtle and causal levels of the mind. Physical purity alone cannot carry the aspirant to higher dimensions because it is related only to the gross body. Beyond the gross body there are several other bodies or planes of existence related to the hidden layers of the mind.

These are subjected to the influence of *samskaras* (latent impressions) which create *sankalpa* and *vikalpa* (thought/counterthought) in the level of the conscious mind. Any disharmony on those levels is immediately transferred to the respective bodies. Just as a physical disease arises out of neglect and carelessness towards the body, there are subtle and

25

causal 'diseases' that build up in the *sukshma sharira* (subtle body) and *karana sharira* (causal body) through carelessness in the way we feel, think, react and interact with life.

We have learned how to combat physical disease, but how are we going to deal with the ailments related to other dimensions of our existence? These ailments are subtle and manifest indirectly. They are only tangible as fears, anxiety, neurosis, psychosis, depression, anger and frustration. When these emotions arise, they not only affect the conscious plane, but even the deeper levels of mind and body. As these are intangible and out of reach, we are unable to find a permanent remedy, so they begin to accumulate and gradually disturb our life and personality.

The body is an extension of the mind. One cannot easily define the limits of the body in relation to the mind as they are intimately interlinked. This creates an interdependence whereby they begin to affect each other. Thus most diseases are either psychosomatic or somopsychic in nature. As a result, the effects of physical disorders eventually disturb the mind and mental disorders create physical diseases.

As the mind is the governing factor over the bodily functions, it becomes necessary to aim at purification on the mental level as well as the physical level. It is in the mind that the germ or virus of infirmity is born and bred. So, when we talk of purification, we should first of all try to understand it in relation to the different layers of the mind. In this respect, let us try to understand what mental purification is. Is it merely the inculcation of virtues such as compassion, mercy and truth, or is there a purification of the mind which transcends even these virtues?

It is in the explanation of this theory that tantra stands apart from other philosophies. Tantra believes that no act or thought is impure in itself. The impurity lies in erroneous perception and judgement. Good and evil cannot be judged on the prejudices of a whimsical society, but on the basis of metaphysical truths. Through personal sadhana it becomes possible to understand impurity and how to combat it.

Without purification on the subtler levels of the mind, it is impossible to attain higher states of awareness, for a mind that is dissipated by thought/counterthought can never achieve one-pointedness and concentration. These oscillating tendencies of the mind can be reduced, either by harmonizing the flow of prana in the body or by disassociating the intellect and ego from the consciousness, so that you become both experiencer and witnesser or *sakshi*.

Purification of the elements

Tattwa shuddhi is unique in that it deals with the process of purification from the grossest to the subtlest level. The first step of purification in tattwa shuddhi sadhana is bathing and cleansing the physical body, applying bhasma (ashes), fasting and diet control. The aspirant has to inculcate a particular attitude even to these mundane acts, for a tantric believes that all aspects of life should be integrated with higher awareness. The manner in which you sit, talk, comb your hair, wash your body, or perform any act, also reflects the inner state of mind. Therefore, the purificatory process in tattwa shuddhi is not just confined to one or two hours of meditation, but extends throughout the twenty-four hours.

This first stage of purification in tattwa shuddhi sadhana should not be understood as 'disciplinary rules', but as a method to heighten your awareness. Thereby, these acts will reflect the inner harmony and joy of existence.

The next stage, which is a more subtle level of purification, is effected through the forces of mind and prana, from which the elements have arisen. These latent inner powers are awakened and directed towards the refinement of the subtle aspect of the tattwas. Refinement of the tattwas on the subtle level, as well as every other level, entails an increase of energy, so that the tattwas themselves vibrate at a harmonious frequency. This induces a state of equilibrium and equipoise, which leads to a deep inner awareness.

27

However, the causal level constituted by the tattwas is the most difficult to purify because it does not come under the influence of the conscious mind and thought. It requires a powerful force of concentrated energy to create a transformation on this level. This is attainable in tattwa shuddhi through repetition of the tattwa bija mantras and visualization of their respective yantras. These have a profound influence on the causal body and unconscious mind, and are able to purge the deep-rooted samskaras and archetypes that obscure the experience of unlimited consciousness.

Just as you bathe every morning to keep yourself clean, similarly, sadhana is like a spiritual bath that cleanses the dross of objective experience. Tattwa shuddhi aims at purification on this dimension of man's consciousness, where the empirical self is completely merged into the transcendental self. This alone is purification according to tantra.

4

Tattwa Shuddhi as a
Part of Tantric Worship

The occidental trend of thought, which has been largely influenced by the guidelines set by the Greek thinkers beginning from Heraclitus and Parmenides, is predominantly objective giving no credence to subjective inner experience. Today this concept is giving way to the idea that consciousness and subjective experience are necessary factors in determining the nature of the cosmos. Tantra, on the other hand, ignored this sharp distinction between subject and object, merging one into the other through a profound understanding of the relation of man's inner subjective experience to the cosmos, thus implying that rituals are not mere symbolic performances, but an enactment of cosmic events.

It is from this notion that the rich imagery and ritualistic part of tantra gradually evolved into a highly complex network of exoteric and esoteric symbols. For every esoteric experience there developed a corresponding exoteric act, which was constructed on the scientific principle that the subjective and objective experience are co-related in more ways than we can imagine. It is for this reason that tantra has emphasized from the beginning the role of conscious awareness of every act that is performed.

Tantra has firmly upheld the view that the consciousness of man, which is forever evolving and expanding, is influenced by the external environment, modes of living, codes of society and ethics, food habits and other such mundane day to day activities. Simultaneously, the external life is also affected by the inner experiences which occur as a result of expanding consciousness. Tantra has, therefore, developed as a ritualistic, highly organized and disciplined exoteric science, as well as an abstract and far-reaching esoteric science.

Tantric ritual

The basic form of exoteric tantric upasana is the ritual of *pooja* (worship) performed for the devis and devatas. For this, temples are constructed along the guidelines of a mandala in which the carved statue of the devi or devata, already invoked with power and life through the ceremony of prana prathistha, is installed. Each devi or devata is bathed, dressed in elaborate clothes and ornaments and offered food or prasad by the temple *poojari*, or worshipper.

On auspicious days, the devi or devata is taken out onto the streets on a specially carved and gilded platform for all to see and admire. In fact, the devi or devata is considered to personify all the characteristics of human behaviour, which the tantras do not consider alien to divine behaviour. There is a special time for bathing, sleeping and eating, during which no one but the temple priest is allowed to enter. Then there are certain foods which are considered more auspicious and favoured. Different devis and devatas have different colour preferences and are dressed accordingly, and so on.

When the devotee goes to the temple for darshan, he offers food, money, clothing, flowers, incense and other such favourable items, prostrates before the image, and meditates on the form of the deity. In this act of darshan, all the senses are stimulated through the profusion of colours, lights, music, mantra and mandala of the deity. In shakti or devi worship, slaughtered animals are offered, as they are considered very propitious and the devotee is greatly benefited by them.

The temple priest who performs the daily worship is chosen from a particular *kula* or family line. His task is to entice the divine powers into the deity, in the presence of the devotee. Thus he must be proficient in the chanting of tantric mantras, along with a thorough knowledge of the procedure of the entire ceremony. The greater the competence of the poojari, the more enthralling and enrapturing is the dramatic event of tantric ritualistic worship.

The ultimate goal of exoteric worship is to reach emancipation through total identification with the deity. One of the first steps in this process is for the priest to consecrate his entire body through the act of *anga nyasa* and *kara nyasa*. This is done by touching different parts of the body with specific fingers, along with repetition of the respective mantras. This is considered an effective method of pratyahara, inducing total sense withdrawal and introversion of mind. A parallel practice can be found in the Christian act of touching the forehead, heart and each shoulder in the sign of the cross.

This is followed by dharana or concentration, by visualizing the five tattwas within the body. Through diffusion of one element into the other, accompanied by symbolic exoteric rites, i.e. *panchopchara*, the priest transforms his entire body/mind into a microcosm of the universe and a fit receptacle for the descent of the divine power.

The entire process is accompanied by the chanting of *kirtan* or devotional songs, by a group of people especially employed for that purpose. Gradually, as the tempo of the music increases, the priest enters a sort of trance, whereby he is merged in dhyana, until he becomes one with the deity and immersed in divine ecstasy.

Once this has been accomplished, the priest places the spirit of the deity, which he has experienced inwardly, into the external statue. Up until this point, the statue is considered an inanimate object, but now it is converted into an aspect of the divine.

This discipline, which is employed by the priest, is also used as an effective means of pratyahara, dharana and dhyana, by aspirants who follow other esoteric tantric practices. It is for this reason that the act of *rishyadi nyasa* (the tantric ceremony) has been modified and is included for the benefit of those who wish to practise tattwa shuddhi as a part of tantric worship.

Rishyadi Nyasa

Pratyahara

Kara nyasa

Hraam Angushtabhyaam Namaha	to the thumbs
Hreem Tarjanibhyaam Swaahaa	to the index fingers
Hroom Madhyamabhyaam Vasat	to the middle fingers
Hraim Anaamikaabhyaam Hoom	to the ring fingers
Hraum Kanisthabhyaam Vausat	to the little fingers
Hrah Karatala-prishtabhyaam Phat	to the palms of the hands

Anga nyasa

Hram Hridayaaya Namaha	to the heart
Hreem Shirasi Swaahaa	to the head
Hroom Shikhaayai Vasat	to the top back portion of the head
Hraim Kavachaaya Hoom	to the protective force; armour
Hraum Netratrayaya Vausat	to the three eyes
Hrah Astraya Phat	to the missile, which alludes to the projecting force of body and mind

Dharana

Tattwa shuddhi

As described in this book.

Panchopchara

Lam to thee of the form of prithvi (earth), I offer gandha (sandal paste).
Vam to thee of the form of apas (water), I offer naivedya (food).
Ram to thee of the form of agni (fire), I offer dipa (light).
Yam to thee of the form of vayu (air), I offer dhupa (incense).
Ham to thee of the form of akasha (ether), I offer phoola (flowers).

Dhyana

Meditation on the ishta devata (personal deity).

5

Prana Shakti

Prana in the body is not moving at random, but in particular patterns, forming vibrations of different frequencies. These various frequencies constitute the physical body as well as subtle organs. On the physical level we can see the separate organs and their constituents, while on a subtler level the organs of energy and their constituents can also be perceived. According to tantra and yoga, these are known as chakras, nadis, kundalini shakti, chitta shakti, prana vayu and panchatattwa.

Prana is both macrocosmic and microcosmic and the substratum of life. Without prana, we would be like decaying corpses with no ability to see, move, hear and so on. There is a charming story in the *Prashnopanishad* to illustrate this:

One day all the *indriyas*, or senses, and prana were having a discussion. The indriyas began to assert, one by one, that if they ceased to function, the *jiva*, or individual soul would perish, and thus its whole existence depended on them. The ears said, "If I withdraw the sense of hearing, then surely humans will not be able to live." The eyes said, "Without sight, a human being is lost in darkness, and cannot live if I withdraw." And so each extolled their own merits.

Finally prana, who had been listening quietly, said, "Why, you self-opinionated fellows, if I were to withdraw myself this moment, none of you would have the strength or capacity to function." So saying, prana began to withdraw, first from the ears, then from the eyes, nose and so on. As they began to lose their grip on the body, the senses began to tremble with fear, and realizing the role of prana, at once ceded their mistake and begged prana to return.

This story illustrates that, without prana, we cannot even blink an eyelid, let alone do all the tasks that we are required to perform throughout life. Prana plays a very vital role in creation and although we are able to function only on account of prana, most of us have not yet been able to develop it to its full potential. The majority of people are so low in prana that they are unable to get through the day without becoming tired, let alone generate extra prana to unfold the inner spiritual experience.

Forms of prana shakti

The cosmic manifestation of prana or *mahaprana* in the individual body is represented by kundalini. The entire cosmic experience from creation to dissolution is embedded within the folds of kundalini. Hence it is known as *atma shakti* or *para shakti* or universal energy. In all living beings, the divine consciousness is first converted into prana or energy and as the kundalini is the reservoir for this magnanimous amount of prana, it is also known as *prana shakti*.

The word kundalini is derived from the term *kunda*, which means 'a pit or cavity'. Kundalini is the inherent energy within the matter of mooladhara chakra, the dormant centre lying in the perineum/cervix. When the full potential of this energy is released, it travels up through the central nervous system in the physical body or sushumna nadi in the pranic body.

Generally however, prana shakti is only partially released from mooladhara chakra through the connecting channels of ida and pingala nadis. Ida and pingala are only capable of conducting a low voltage of energy: they vitalize the mind and body, but not to its full potential. Only the full force of kundalini shakti, or prana shakti or atma shakti can awaken the entire conscious and vital functions. Pingala nadi also channels prana shakti, but we should not confuse the two meanings of the words prana shakti. On one level, it is *para* (transcendental) in the form of kundalini shakti; on the other it is *pinda* (microcosmic) in the form of prana shakti, which is channelled through pingala.

Prana shakti also manifests as six main centres or chakras or storehouses of prana, which are located along the spinal column. The lowest chakra in the energy circuit, *mooladhara*, is situated in the perineum of men and the cervix of women, and connects to the coccygeal plexus. The next chakra, *swadhisthana*, is two fingers-width above mooladhara, and corresponds to the sacral plexus. Above this is *manipura*, behind the navel, which corresponds to the solar plexus. In the spinal column, in the region of the heart, is *anahata*, which connects to the cardiac plexus. In the middle of the neck is *vishuddhi chakra*, which corresponds to the cervical plexus. At the very top of the spinal cord, at the medulla oblongata, is *ajna chakra*, which connects with the pineal gland in the physical body.

Each chakra is constituted of one basic element. Within mooladhara is prithvi (earth) tattwa; in swadhisthana, apas (water) tattwa; in manipura, agni (fire) tattwa; in anahata, vayu (air) tattwa; in vishuddhi, akasha (ether) tattwa. The particular element which governs each chakra indicates the level at which the chakra vibrates and operates.

Our entire range of consciousness, thoughts and actions is governed by the activities of these chakras. The chakras are energized by pingala nadi and fully activated by the ascent of kundalini. As long as they are not fully activated, we are limited in every action and experience. In tattwa shuddhi sadhana, these chakras are directly influenced by concentration on each tattwa.

Prana shakti as energy fields

In order to control the functions of the body, prana shakti also manifests as the five major *prana vayus* or pranic air currents, known as *prana*, *apana*, *samana*, *udana* and *vyana*.

Apart from these, there are five *upapranas* or subsidiary pranas. Together these ten pranas control the entire processes of the human body, such as digestion, evacuation, sneezing, blinking, talking, moving, breathing.

Out of these, the two most influential vayus are prana and apana. Prana is the inward moving force which is said to create a field moving upwards from the navel to the throat. Apana is the outward moving force which is said to create a field, moving downwards from the navel to the anus. Both prana and apana move spontaneously in the body, but are controlled through tantric and yogic practices. In the Upanishads it is said that a method has to be employed to reverse these opposite moving forces of prana and apana, so that they unite with samana in the navel centre, the result of which is the awakening of kundalini.

Through this entire network of physical, subtle and cosmic manifestations of prana, prana shakti creates, sustains and ultimately destroys the notion of individual existence in human beings.

Prana shakti as Devi

Shakti in the transcendental realm is beyond conceptualization in terms of gender. However, in the immanent realm, shakti is depicted as the goddess Devi. The word shakti itself denotes a female principle and around this concept developed a whole cluster of goddesses, each of whom represents the supreme shakti, either fully as *poorna shakti* (complete manifestation), or in part as *amsa roopini* (partial manifestation). These aspects of shakti are several and each of them represents a different aspect or power within the individual. The poorna shaktis are Kali, Durga, Lakshmi, Saraswati and Parvati; the amsa roopinis are many, some of whom are Dakini, Rakini, Lakini, Kakini, Sakini and Hakini.

In the human body, the poorna shaktis are represented by the ascending kundalini and the amsa roopinis are represented by the opening of the chakras. Just as watering the plants for a few days causes all the flowers to bloom,

Prana Shakti as Devi
(visualized in red)

similarly, kundalini shakti, when it awakens, provides the energy and nourishment for activating the amsa roopinis to unfold their total potential.

Mandala of prana shakti

In tattwa shuddhi, kundalini as prana shakti is symbolized as a beautiful goddess. This tradition of symbolizing every aspect of human existence as a mandala is an essential part of tantra. These mandalas are more than just symbols; they represent man's unknown subconscious and unconscious. It is believed that concentration on these forms detonates the samskaras or archetypes that obscure creativity and genius.

The mandala of prana shakti is created in tattwa shuddhi to influence this process. The different aspects of her form are not chosen arbitrarily, rather they have been carefully selected to express particular levels of consciousness. The colour of her skin is 'red like the rising sun', which indicates the boons she can grant. Meditation on Devi in red is done for conquest over the lower self and subjugation of all the forces which keep one within the clutches of samskaras or worldly life. Red is a primary colour which represents *rajoguna* or the quality of dynamism. As prana is a vital force motivating action in all living beings, the colour red also alludes to the dynamic tendencies of prana.

Her six hands denote her high level of efficiency in every act she performs and each object she holds in her six hands represents victory over different aspects of human existence. The goad is symbolic of the eradication of dwesha or dislike and the noose symbolizes a conquest over the different forms of raga or desire. The bow depicts the mind in a state of total one-pointedness or concentration; the five arrows represent the five tanmatras, five tattwas, five jnanendriyas, and five karmendriyas which are brought under control by a concentrated mind. The trident stands as a symbol of the three gunas in a state of equipoise and balance; and, lastly, the skull with the dripping blood is symbolic of dissolution and annihilation of the ego.

38

Her smiling and benevolent countenance depicts prana shakti as one who willingly grants boons, thus ensuring the success of dhyana or meditation done on her form. Her three open eyes represent vision into every realm and the third eye, in particular, indicates her cosmic vision. The lotus on which she is seated denotes the unfoldment of divine powers or siddhis.

The practice of tattwa shuddhi deals with prana shakti in its diverse aspects. Moreover, as the tattwas are created by the vibration of prana at varying frequencies, we pay obeisance to prana shakti, who plays a vital role in our evolution from consciousness to matter and matter to consciousness. Meditation on prana shakti is the culminating point in the practice of tattwa shuddhi.

6

Evolution of the Elements

Tantra says that the macrocosmos is inherent in the microcosmos. Thus, the whole law of cosmic manifestation and dissolution is inherent in each individual. Just as the physical and mental characteristics of an individual are inherent in the DNA molecule, similarly, the molecular structure of a human being contains the prototype of the cosmic properties. This cosmic experience of creation and dissolution is symbolized in the form of kundalini shakti.

Kundalini is para shakti, the subtlest form of energy as well as the inseparable part of pure consciousness. Although energy and consciousness have separated and diversified to give rise to the whole creation, they are forever striving to unite in the physical body, in order to re-experience the cosmic unity from which they evolved.

Tantric symbology has employed several images to indicate these two universal aspects within the physical body. Shakti or energy, lying latent at the base of the spine, is depicted in the form of a coiled serpent, known as kundalini. Shiva or consciousness resides in the highest spiritual centre, sahasrara chakra, which is situated at the top of the head in the form of a crystal shivalingam. As the supreme energy of kundalini is awakened through the practice of tantra, the consciousness is freed from the matter of the body.

This happens in several stages and prior to the ultimate union of energy and consciousness (shiva/shakti) in sahasrara chakra, they unite at various levels in the chakras. It is the final union in sahasrara chakra which eventually replicates the original notion of unity between Shiva and Shakti preceding creation. Thus we can grasp how the entire cosmic process, from unity to diversity and back to unity, is inherent within each of us.

Tantric philosophy postulates that the universe of matter and energy has evolved out of primordial nature or shakti who represents pure energy. Her cosmic counterpart and co-creator is shiva, or pure consciousness, who exists as conscious intelligence distinct from her and her derivatives. In the original state, shiva is forever immanent and eternal but inactive, as opposed to shakti who is forever immanent and eternal but active. Shakti has the inherent potential to create and is, therefore, known as the root matrix of creation or *moola prakriti*.

Although shiva and shakti momentarily separate to give rise to the individual consciousness, in their cosmic manifestation, they are forever co-existing, side by side. So there is both a cosmic and individual aspect of shiva and shakti. This individual aspect of shiva/shakti appears as a dual force only due to the obscuring power of maya, the illusory force inherent in the shakti principle.

Shiva and shakti together give rise to the *avyakta* or unmanifest cosmos as well as the *vyakta* or manifest universe. The first manifestations of the cosmic process of creation are known as nada, bindu and kaala. *Nada* literally means 'vibration'. As a part of the avyakta or unmanifest creation, it exists as the cosmic vibration. In the vyakta or manifest creation it exists as sound of varying frequencies. *Bindu* represents a point or nucleus, and *kaala* is a ray or force which emanates from the nucleus or bindu.

The parallel drawn by science is that of a particle and wave of energy. The great controversy as to whether light is composed of particles or waves, which has tormented scientists, remains unresolved to this day. The question has never been answered by science, except by stating that it is both.

Tantra has defined that both particle (bindu) and ray or wave (kaala) exist. Moreover, it has asserted that this fundamental dualism affects the entire gamut of physical creation.

The cosmic manifestation of shiva and shakti as nada, bindu and kaala interact and give rise to the gross and subtle elements of which man is composed. In tantra it is considered that the human body, on the gross, subtle and causal levels, is composed of thirty-six elements. These thirty-six tattwas cover the entire spectrum of human existence and experience. However, fifteen supplementary elements are also included in the ultimate definition of the human form, thus making a total of fifty-one elements, corresponding with the fifty-one letters of the Sanskrit alphabet. These supplementary elements consist of the *sapta dhatus* or seven humours in the body, the *pancha vayu* or five vital airs, and the *triguna* or three basic qualities.

In tattwa shuddhi we deal with only twenty-five of these tattwas. However, in order to have a broader perspective of what we are made up of, it is necessary to understand the entire process of creation or *srishti* from the tantric standpoint. The thirty-six tattwas are classified into three categories of shiva tattwa, vidya tattwa and atma tattwa.

Shiva tattwa

The shiva tattwa is composed of five pure elements which are related to absolute consciousness. The first two of the shiva tattwas consist of shiva as the pure consciousness or *chit*, in union with shakti as the pure energy or *chit shakti*. Inherent in chit shakti are three creative aspects known as: *ichchha* – energy of will; *kriya* – energy of action; and *jnana* – energy of knowledge.

These five unconditioned tattwas are a part of the macrocosmic or universal consciousness, which are symbolized in the union of shiva/shakti or the cosmic experience. The three aspects of ichchha, kriya and jnana, inherent in the chit shakti, remain dormant until the point of creation. Until the exact moment of creation, these five elements that comprise the shiva tattwa, remain unified as one or whole; there is no division or diversity. The first indication of division in this unity leads to the development of the vidya tattwas, which are a part of the microcosmic consciousness.

Vidya tattwa

The vidya tattwa, composed of seven subtle elements, is related to both absolute consciousness and veiled consciousness. It is the unconditioned and conditioned elements of the microcosmic consciousness. The development of the vidya tattwa is responsible for the limitations which begin to manifest on the otherwise unconditioned tattwas. At this stage, shiva or consciousness remains complete in itself, but is enveloped by the veiling power inherent in chit shakti, i.e. *maya*. Here maya operates through five limiting aspects known as the kanchukas. *Kanchuka* literally means 'sheath' or 'envelope', and together they act like the shell which obscures the kernel. Each kanchuka limits the cosmic power of shiva/shakti in one aspect.

These limiting aspects, or kanchukas, born out of maya are:

1. *Kalaa* – that which limits the force of kriya shakti or the power to do all.
2. *Avidya vidya* – that which limits the force of jnana shakti or the power to know all.
3. *Raga* – that which limits the force of ichchha shakti by creating desire and attachment, thus giving rise to unceasing discontentment.
4. *Kaala* – that which limits perpetual existence by creating the notion of time, related to the changes in life, namely: birth, growth, ripening, waning and perishing.
5. *Niyati* – that which limits free will (*purushartha*) by creating the notion of fate and destiny, thus binding the individual to the endless cycle of birth and death.

Thus, in this stage we see the omnipresence, omniscience and omnipotence of the shiva/shakti unity, veiled by the power of maya to create the notion of duality. What this

43

really implies is that, although in the state preceding creation shiva and shakti existed as one unit of consciousness, during the process of creation they appear diversified through the power of maya. In actual fact they always remain what they are, and in human beings their unity is represented by paramatma consciousness, which to the jivatma appears different from itself.

Subjectively this process of maya results in the dichotomy of subject and object, in contrast to the unified experience of shiva and shakti, and objectively it results in the creation of the various physical forms of which the universe is composed. It is at this point in the scheme of evolution that dualities, divisions and opposites come into existence. This leads to the development of the atma tattwas or conditioned elements which constitute the material universe. In the practice of tattwa shuddhi, it is these conditioned elements or atma tattwas with which we deal.

Atma tattwas

The *atma tattwa* is composed of twenty-five elements related to veiled consciousness. They are the conditioned elements of the individual consciousness. At this stage of development, the macrocosmic elements are diversified by the power of the vidya tattwas to manifest into the physical universe. At first, the shiva tattwa transforms itself into the *purusha tattwa* or pure consciousness in man, representing the innermost focal point in each person. The shakti tattwa transforms itself into the *prakriti tattwa* or kinetic principle, representing the dormant energy or kundalini shakti which is present at the base of the spine, although in this physical form the original power of shiva/shakti is forever limited by maya.

The development after the manifestation of prakriti is known as *parinama* or real evolution, for it is now that the consciousness is divided into time and space, or subjective and objective self. What is spoken of in terms of development prior to this is in actual fact a condition in which shakti assumes various aspects with a view to create, but without

Evolution of the Individual Elements

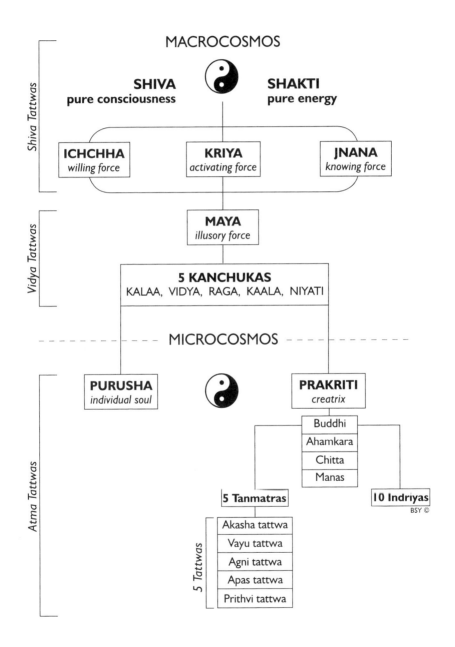

manifestation. Thus previously, shakti tattwa, whilst retaining its original state, assumes the aspect of nada, bindu, kalaa, ichchha, jnana, kriya and maya.

The three inherent aspects of chit shakti, namely ichchha, kriya and jnana, now transform themselves into the three gunas: tamas, rajas and sattwa. Ichchha shakti is transformed into *tamoguna*, which represents inertia; kriya shakti is transformed into *rajoguna*, which represents action, and jnana shakti is transformed into *sattwa guna*, which represents radiant knowledge. Together these three gunas rule the whole span of human life, and dominate the action of the next differentiated stage: buddhi, ahamkara, manas and chitta, which constitute the inner instrument of man through which consciousness acts.

Antah karana (inner tool)

1. *Buddhi* – also known as *mahat*, is the highest intelligence, which manifests its full potential under the influence of sattwa guna.
2. *Ahamkara* – the principle of individuality or ego, which emphasizes the existence of the self.
3. *Manas* – the mind or mental faculty, of thought/counterthought.
4. *Chitta* – the collection of past impressions or samskaras.

It is at this point that matter begins to dominate spirit, giving rise to the multiplicity of creation. Ahamkara gives rise to the gross elements, indriyas, *tanmatras* (subtle essences) and tattwas which comprise the physical body. The gross tattwas, which are grouped into numbers of five, are as follows:

Tanmatras (subtle essences)

1. *Shabda* – sound; the subtle essence of akasha tattwa.
2. *Sparsha* – touch; the subtle essence of vayu tattwa.
3. *Roopa* – form; the subtle essence of agni tattwa.
4. *Rasa* – taste; the subtle essence of apas tattwa.
5. *Gandha* – smell; the subtle essence of prithvi tattwa.

Tattwas (elements)

1. *Akasha* – ether; responsible for void and space.
2. *Vayu* – air; responsible for perpetual motion.
3. *Agni* – fire; responsible for heat.
4. *Apas* – water; responsible for fluidity.
5. *Prithvi* – earth; responsible for cohesion, weight.

Jnanendriyas (organs of knowledge)

1. *Srotra* – ears, the auditory sense; perception of sound.
2. *Twacha* – skin, the tactile sense; perception of touch or feeling.
3. *Chakshu* – eyes, the optic sense; perception of form.
4. *Jihwa* – tongue, the gustatory sense; perception of taste.
5. *Ghrana* – nose, the olfactory sense; perception of smell.

Karmendriyas (organs of action)

1. *Vak* – speech; the organ of articular expression.
2. *Pani* – hand; the organ of grasping.
3. *Pada* – foot; the organ of locomotion.
4. *Upastha* – reproductory organ; the organ of regeneration.
5. *Payu* – anal region; the organ of evacuation.

In the practice of tattwa shuddhi we consciously recreate the process of evolution and involution, experiencing each element separately but as a part of the intricate whole. We begin to perceive the interdependence of the elements and how they play a vital role in the interplay of consciousness and energy. Thereby the twenty-five elements are refined.

7

Antah Karana:
Individual Mind

Antah karana is a combination of two Sanskrit words. *Antah* is inner, and *karana* is tool or instrument. Antah karana is thus the inner tool or instrument of man. It is comprised of four faculties: buddhi (intellect), ahamkara (ego), manas (thought/counterthought) and chitta (memory). According to tantra and yoga, these four principles constitute the medium through which the consciousness acts.

Antah karana distinguishes human beings from the plant, animal and mineral kingdoms. In these lower forms of life, antah karana exists in a dormant and tamasic seed state. These creations of nature do not operate from the level of intellect, discrimination, thought or ego, but from the level of pure instinct. For example, a dog will instinctively prefer meat to vegetables. He does not consciously discriminate one from the other; it is a natural instinctive process which governs his body.

However, in the case of man, this faculty has gradually evolved to its present capacity. Man has emerged victorious over all other forms of life by the strength of this inner faculty, which has given him the power to reason, think, plan, remember and enact.

However, the intellectual supremacy of man does not in any way complement the full potential of the antah karana. It is just a mere glimpse of the power that it contains. If the performance of this instrument reaches its full capacity, man cannot only control the inferior creations of nature, but also the latent forces within himself, which have the inherent power to create, preserve and destroy. Thus he would become a co-creator or an instrument, one with nature, replicating her cosmic processes. The yogis, who have attained the power to do so, achieved this rare feat by exploring the mysteries of this inner instrument, the antah karana.

The consciousness of man, acting through the antah karana, interprets, classifies, conjectures, perceives and cognizes all data related to the past, present and future experiences. Everything you feel, see, do or speak, is a part of what is stored there. There is a part of antah karana that has knowledge not only of this life and experiences related to it but knowledge of the whole universe and cosmos.

However, due to the grossness of one's awareness, the full potential of knowledge remains dormant and unmanifested, and it will remain this way unless one begins to refine the antah karana. Refinement of antah karana implies tuning it to the high frequencies of pure energy and consciousness, so that we become aware that, in fact, what we are refining is a creation of that same energy and consciousness.

The physical evolution of man today stands complete. He may grow shorter or taller, fatter or thinner, but the next stage of evolution belongs to the realm of consciousness. Sri Aurobindo talks about a 'superhuman race', when man has achieved this state of higher mind. 'Superhuman race' is a term which implies mental, emotional, rational and, above all, spiritual development of man at its zenith. At present, these faculties in us are only at the teething stage and we are still grappling with their complexities. Much of the success we can have in this area depends on our ability to purify, illumine and unify the functions of the antah karana.

The antah karana acts like a very fine transmitter which receives and transmits impressions. The clarity and precision with which it performs this act depends entirely on how refined your instrument has become. If it is tuned to the gross vibrations, then that is what the transmitter will reflect.

49

However, if it is tuned to the subtleties of cosmic vibration, then not only can you discover the underlying mysteries behind your own existence, but also the enigma which is underlying the whole cosmos.

Man is not a separate entity, suspended between cause and event. Rather, he is an integral part of the cosmic plan that has a role for each and every speck of creation. The antah karana plays a vital part in our pursuit to understand this role.

This infinitely subtle instrument is what we ourselves have built through our fine sense of imagery during our journey through many successive incarnations. Thus the antah karana contains the impressions which we carry lifetime after lifetime. Like a musical instrument, the antah karana is sensitive enough to pick up the subtlest vibrations, which it continues to do irrespective of our conscious knowledge. You may not be consciously aware of certain impressions that are forming within you, but your antah karana keeps vigil at all times.

It is your antah karana that decides your course of action, depending on past experience or knowledge. What is recorded there may never reveal itself to you, unless the clarity of cosmic awareness and the inner ear and eye, which can comprehend the subtle vibrations of cosmic sound and vision, are attained. Therefore, we have not only to discover what is stored in the antah karana, but also learn how to control it. Tantra is the only science which has given us the answer.

Antah karana is the tool through which consciousness is playing its cosmic game or *lila*. Consciousness is the same in everyone – pure, effulgent and radiant. How it expresses itself depends on the precision, clarity and perception of the medium through which it plays its game. The same idea, the same thought, the same action may occur in two different people, but the interpretation, enactment and culminating results will depend entirely on the level of mind, intellect and ego of each of the persons.

Dimensions of the mind

In yoga, the mind is classified into four stages: *jagriti* (conscious), *swapna* (subconscious), *sushupti* (unconscious) and *turiya* (transcendental). Thus yoga speaks of the fourfold mind as opposed to modern psychology, which has limited itself to just three forms of awareness: conscious, subconscious and unconscious.

The antah karana functions through the conscious, subconscious and unconscious realms, creating gross, subtle and causal experiences. As the antah karana has evolved out of a combination of the three gunas: sattwa, rajas and tamas, the quality of experience is largely determined by the pervading influence of these cosmic principles. Manas, chitta, buddhi and ahamkara behave differently under the sway of sattwa, as opposed to rajas and tamas, and thus manifest differently in the three states of awareness.

Manas and chitta, being a part of the conscious and subconscious awareness, dominate the actions and thoughts in the jagriti and swapna states. Buddhi and ahamkara are present in varying degrees of refinement in the jagriti, swapna and sushupti states. However, as these faculties have evolved out of each other and from the same principle of shakti, their interdependence and invasion on each other are inevitable.

It is evident that in these three states of consciousness, antah karana is under the sway of the three gunas, modifying itself to the guna which is predominant at any particular time. But in the fourth stage, turiya or transcendental awareness, the gunas cease to exert any influence, and thus the awareness is transported beyond the fluctuations of antah karana that exist in the preceding three states. This is only achieved by developing the full capacity of the antah karana through sadhana.

In the practice of tattwa shuddhi, the role of antah karana is rendered clear. The aspirant is able to perceive the functionings of this powerful tool and the method of directing its full force towards spiritual attainment.

51

Buddhi

Buddhi, which is also known as mahat or the great principle, is said to be the faculty closest to pure consciousness. When buddhi is turned towards the enjoyment of sensorial pleasures, it causes bondage of the soul, but when it is endowed with dispassion, the soul turns towards liberation. In daily life, it is buddhi that motivates you to act according to your dharma (vocation). Any act judged with precision and accuracy is on account of the power and influence of buddhi or the higher intellect.

At a higher level, buddhi reflects itself through *prajna* (intuition) and *vairagya* (dispassion). Although these sublime qualities are inherent in buddhi, under the influence of maya and due to its association with ego, senses and the three gunas, these qualities are often altered.

The characteristics of the sattwic buddhi are wisdom, dispassion, reasoning, endurance, serenity, self-control, discrimination and contemplation. In the sattwic state, buddhi is without oscillation and assumes the role of sakshi (the witnesser). Due to the influence of rajas, defects arise. As a result, buddhi is unable to discriminate, and the decisions are often contaminated by false knowledge and avidya or ignorance. Tamasic buddhi comes under the sway of ego and is clouded by false information and false judgements.

In the practice of tattwa shuddhi, we meditate on the sattwic nature of buddhi so that the tamasic and rajasic tendencies, which are not its true nature and which prevent sattwic buddhi from operating, are removed. Thus the experience of being the silent witnesser or sakshi is accentuated.

Ahamkara

Aham is 'I' and ahamkara is ego or that which experiences 'I-ness'. Unified existence and unity at all levels is torn asunder at the birth of ego and one perceives its separation from the rest of creation. Within ego is contained the germ of individuality and thus a process of identification and attachment to objects and persons ensues. Ahamkara pervades each and every pore of your being. Its manifestation is extremely subtle and the web it spins so ensnaring that one remains bound in its clutches life after life.

Ahamkara or ego forms the nucleus of existence within an individual. It is only on account of the ego that you relate to things around you. If there was no ego, you would be just like a plant or vegetable having no knowledge of your existence. This is the paradox of creation, that on the one hand ego binds you to the plane of objective experience, and on the other it exists as the nucleus which has to be exploded to awaken unified existence.

In the conscious state or jagriti, ego operates through the gross body, i.e. the senses and thinking mind. In the subconscious state or swapna, the ego operates through the astral body and dream. When you are in deep sleep, sushupti, the ego retires into seed state in the causal body, but in meditation it is in the form of inner awareness. Ahamkara is so deeply embedded that it even remains through the stages of savikalpa samadhi.

The functions of ahamkara are affected by the three qualities of sattwa, rajas and tamas. Sattwic ahamkara is responsible for the notion that 'I am', and acts as a catalyst in the process of self-realization. Ahamkara stirs up samskaras or latent impressions from the subconscious mind, but under the influence of sattwa or balance it temporarily withdraws this function.

Rajasic ahamkara is a dynamic force which kindles 'I-ness' in the individual, causing intense activity and restlessness. Ultimately, it leads to dissipation of thought and action. Tamasic ahamkara intensifies the painful and negative samskaras, thus causing doubt, apprehension, fear and procrastination.

Ahamkara can be considered the source of both limitation and liberation of the jiva or individual soul. Although it stays with one a long time on one's life's journey, through sadhana one is gradually able to refine its negative forces. By the practice of tattwa shuddhi, we become more aware of the subtlety of ego, thus making it easier to disidentify with its lower functions.

Manas and chitta

Manas and chitta represent the external mind and mindstuff, i.e. the stuff which is apparent in waking and dream states. Chitta is the seat of all experiences in the form of samskaras, archetypes and memory. Manas or thought/counterthought is its vehicle or means of expression. Manas and chitta do not simply function by themselves. They are guided by the logical reasoning of buddhi and the assertive tendencies of ahamkara.

The inherent quality of manas is to be dominated by rajoguna. It is forever distracted and diversified. Just as a little child picks up a toy but soon leaves it for another, similarly it is the tendency of manas to continuously jump from one thought to another.

This rajasic tendency is altered when manas comes under the sway of ahamkara to a state of tamas, and transformed when it comes under the sway of buddhi to a state of equilibrium or sattwa. Thus ahamkara and buddhi operate through manas, drawing upon the contents of past impressions stored in the chitta to create an experience of happiness or unhappiness, pain or pleasure.

The activity of manas changes constantly under the influence of the three gunas. In the state of sattwa, manas becomes steady, one-pointed and concentrated. Manas, influenced by rajas, activates the senses and unbalances the intellect. Tamasic manas makes the intellect and senses lazy and inactive.

Chitta is sometimes referred to as the higher mind or intellect, but here we are only concerned with its function as memory. Under the influence of sattwa, the sense impressions contained within chitta recede, so that the consciousness remains undisturbed. Through the influence of rajoguna, the rajasic samskaras are awakened in chitta in the form of *vikalpa* (imagination) and *viparyaya* (false knowledge). In this state, chitta contains both types of samskaras of knowledge and ignorance, passion and dispassion.

When tamas influences chitta, undesirable samskaras well up. Thus the individual is clouded by *vasanas* (deep-rooted desires) pushing all the good samskaras into obscurity. It is only possible to eliminate irrelevant samskaras through the process of reflection, dharana and dhyana. Perfection in the practice of tattwa shuddhi leads the aspirant to one-pointed concentration and meditation, so awareness becomes free to reflect on the nature of the tattwas.

We have to realize that the main pathway to attainment of self-realization lies through the antah karana. In order to gain full control over the direction of its development, we will have to turn to tantric and yogic sadhana. In the practice of tattwa shuddhi, we use the latent forces of antah karana to direct the awareness away from gross experience towards higher experience.

8

Panchatattwa:
the Five Elements

Tantra stipulates that all matter is composed of a combination of five tattwas or bhutas, i.e. elements. The *Shiva Swarodaya* explains that, "Creation takes place due to the tattwas and by them it is sustained." In the *Tantraraja Tantra*, Shakti asks Shiva, "Where do all the tattwas exist, in the body or out of it?" Shiva replies that the tattwas permeate the entire body and mind. Everything you do and think is under the influence of these tattwas. Therefore, in yoga it is necessary to know how the tattwas behave and in which manner they can be controlled and utilized.

The five tattwas are known as akasha or ether, vayu or air, agni or fire, apas or water, prithvi or earth. However, these tattwas should not be mistaken for physical or chemical elements. Prithvi is not the earth we see around us. Water is not the water we drink or bath with. Nor is fire that which we burn to keep warm and so on. Rather they should be regarded as a consequence of light and sound emanations which are created by different energy or pranic vibrations.

The science of astrology has verified that the first four of these tattwas or elements, earth, water, fire and air, have a major influence on our personality, mind, emotions and destiny, but it has failed to include the most subtle and important element, i.e. ether, which is responsible for spiritual experience. However, the science of tantra and yoga, which has examined the tattwas in greater detail, has clearly stated that man is composed of, and continuously subject to, the influence of these five tattwas.

The tantric texts enumerate a complete science of the tattwas, according to which the practitioner can not only predict the future, but also control the results accruing from his actions throughout the day. Of course, this should not be the aim for which we strive to attain this knowledge. It is merely to indicate the intimate connection between the tattwas and the entire structure of your life, so that it is even possible for you to alter your destiny through tattwa jnana, i.e. knowledge of the elements.

These five tattwas form part of a connected series in which each successive tattwa is derived from its predecessor. The first tattwa to evolve is akasha, undifferentiated matter containing an infinite amount of potential energy. Therefore, akasha is the subtle state when both energy and matter exist in their dormant potential state in the bosom of consciousness.

As the energy inherent in the particles of akasha begins to vibrate, movement is created and vayu tattwa emerges in the form of air. The particles of vayu have the greatest freedom of movement and, therefore, vayu tattwa is seen as an all-pervading motion. Due to the excessive movement of energy in vayu, heat is generated, which acts as the cause for the emergence of the next tattwa, agni.

In agni tattwa the movement of energy is less than that of vayu tattwa. This decrease of motion enables agni tattwa to dispel part of its radiative heat and thus cool into the apas or water tattwa. With the birth of apas tattwa, the complete freedom of movement of vayu tattwa and the partial freedom of movement of agni tattwa are lost, and the particles of these elements are confined within a definite space, moving only within a small radius.

The last tattwa, prithvi, evolves out of a further decrease in energy vibration, which causes apas to solidify into prithvi. Here even the limited freedom of movement within apas is lost. Each particle of prithvi has its own place, and any vibration is confined to the space it occupies.

Creation of matter

In order to create matter, these five elements undergo a process of permutation and combination, which is an intricate process of nature. Each element is divided into two equal parts. The second part of each element is further divided into four equal parts (i.e. one eighth of the whole). Then the first part (one half of the element) combines with one eighth of each of the other four elements to constitute matter, i.e. half of ether combines with one eighth of each of the other four elements and likewise the same process takes place with each of the elements.

This is known as the process of quintuplication, and after this, permutation and combination takes place. This process of converting subtle elements into gross matter is termed as *panchikara* and is responsible for the physical body and the entire universe. It is stated that in the physical body these elements are present in the ratio 5:4:3:2:1, prithvi occupying a greater portion of the body, followed by water, fire, air and ether respectively, in lesser proportions. These proportions determine our individual physical, mental and spiritual capacity.

Different permutations and combinations produce different results. For the purpose of explanation, let us say that if you subtract or add some of the essential ingredients that combine to form a man, and slightly alter their permutation and combination, the result could well be an ape, an elephant or a goat – who knows? The exact combinations and proportions of existent matter are known only to Nature and this has remained one of her secrets. If we are able to divulge this secret, it would not be long before matter would be composed and destroyed in a laboratory at the behest of a scientist.

This is not hard to believe. The process of telephoto graphy or satellite transmission is based on the same principle. In order to broadcast events from one country to another, they are transmitted, not as photographs, but as sound and light waves. Later these waves are reassembled to reproduce the exact picture which was transmitted. Soon it may even be possible to do the same with animate and inanimate objects.

For example, if you had to travel from the earth to Jupiter (which is many light-years away), you would first be converted into light and sound waves, and after you reached your destination you would be reassembled into your own form. It sounds bizarre, but if you can grasp the concept, then it will be easy to understand exactly what your body is composed of and how it has condensed into the form that you perceive.

In the scheme of evolution, these five tattwas originated out of the tamas predominating tanmatras. A tanmatra is an abstract quality through which the tattwa is perceived. Thus akasha is perceived through shabda tanmatra (sound), vayu through sparsha tanmatra (touch or feel), agni through roopa tanmatra (form or vision), apas through rasa tanmatra (taste), and prithvi through gandha tanmatra (smell).

These tanmatras or root principles of sense perception are intricately linked with the senses or indriyas through which they cognize and act. The indriyas are of two kinds: jnanendriyas (organs of cognition) and karmendriyas (organs of action). However, the indriyas are not sufficient in themselves, but are dependent on sankalpa/vikalpa, (selection and rejection), qualities of the mind. Moreover, the sensations produced through the indriyas are also subject to ahamkara, which identifies them as personal experience, and buddhi, which cognizes all experiences.

Thus all the tattwas should be regarded as an extension of pure consciousness and not as individual entities existing separately. It should be remembered that in the course of evolution, subtle states give rise to grosser states, and each grosser state has for its cause the preceding element. Thus, the cause is an essential part of the effect.

Akasha tattwa, which evolves from the akasha tanmatra, does not contain the qualities of the other four tattwas, as they are grosser than it. Out of akasha evolves vayu, which is made up of both akasha tanmatra and vayu tanmatra. From vayu arises the tattwa of agni, which contains the akasha, vayu and agni tanmatras. Agni later develops into apas, which contains akasha, vayu, agni and apas tanmatras. In the last tattwa, prithvi, the qualities of all five tattwas are combined.

Thus it can be found that the qualities attributed to the tattwas are intermingled, and although each tattwa has a predominant characteristic, it also imbibes a portion of the qualities of the tattwa from which it has evolved. Ether has the quality of sound; air has the quality of both sound and touch, although touch is predominant. Agni has form as its predominating quality, with traces of sound and touch. Apas is taste predominated, but also has the qualities of sound, touch and form. In prithvi, though smell is the predominating quality, sound, touch, form and taste are also present. Therefore, it is easy to ascertain that prithvi, due to its wide range of sense perception, is the grossest tattwa to perceive, and ether, which has only sound as its medium, is the subtlest.

These five tattwas, which compose the total matter in your body, were reduced to their grossest form in your mother's womb. Their grossness has to be refined, just as petroleum has to be refined into petrol. The aim of tattwa shuddhi is to enable this refinement, so that the grossness of the tattwas is transformed into the experiences related to the subtler tattwas. Just as a scientist is able to observe the minutest form of life under a microscope, similarly, in tattwa shuddhi the aspirant is led to a world where matter is perceived, not in its dense form, but as consciousness.

In the *Yoga Sutras* of Sage Patanjali, it is stated that every tattwa has five characteristics, and in order to attain mastery over the tattwas, the aspirant has to practise *samyama* (a spontaneous combination of concentration, meditation, samadhi) on these characteristics. Sage Patanjali has termed this process as *bhuta jaya* or mastery over the elements.

The first characteristic of these five tattwas is the gross form, which is related to the experiences attained through the senses as sound, touch, form, taste and smell. The second is the quality of the elements. For example, the solidity of earth, the liquidity of water, the heat of fire, the movement and vibration

Characteristics of the Five Elements

Characteristic	Earth	Water	Fire	Air	Ether
Nature	heavy	cool	hot	erratic	mixed
Quality	weight; cohesion	fluidity; contraction	heat; expansion	motion; movement	diffused; space-giving
Colour	yellow	white	red	blue-grey	blackish
Shape	quadrangular	crescent moon	triangular	hexagonal	bindu/dot
Chakra	mooladhara	swadhisthana	manipura	anahata	vishuddhi
Mantra	lam	vam	ram	yam	ham
Tanmatra	smell	taste	sight	touch	sound
Function in body	skin; blood vessels bone construction	all bodily fluids	appetite; thirst sleep	muscular expansion, contraction	emotions; passions
Karmendriya	anus	reproductive organ	feet	hands	vocal cords
Jnanendriya	nose	tongue	eyes	skin	ears
Location*	toes to knees	knees to navel	navel to heart	heart to mid-eyebrows	mid-eyebrows to top of head
Mental state	ahamkara (ego)	buddhi (discrimination)	manas (thought/counter-thought)	chitta (psychic content)	prajna (intuition)
Kosha	annamaya	pranamaya	manomaya	vijnanamaya	anandamaya
Prana vayu	apana	prana	samana	udana	vyana
Loka	bhu	bhuvar	swar	maha	jana
Direction	east	west	south	north	middle & above

*As in Tattwa Shuddhi

of air and the vacancy or spaciousness of ether. The third is the subtle aspect, which is related to the subtleties of the tanmatras. Just as there is the gross range of sense perception, there is a subtler state, in which the tattwas are experienced as subtle sounds, subtle touch, subtle form, subtle taste and subtle smell. These subtle forms are often termed as psychic visions and are the supersensitive states of sense perception.

The fourth aspect of the tattwas is related to the three gunas: sattwa, rajas and tamas. These three gunas representing radiance, activity and inertia are an integral part of the five tattwas. Thus akasha, as well as vayu, agni, apas and prithvi, are considered to be present in the body in their sattwic, rajasic and tamasic states. In order to attain spiritual experience, the aspirant has to subdue the tamasic and rajasic states of the tattwas and transform them into the radiance of sattwa. This transformation is what the practice of tattwa shuddhi enables.

The fifth aspect of the tattwas is known as *arthavattwa* and denotes the purpose of the tattwas. The scriptures unanimously claim that it is for the enjoyment and liberation of consciousness from matter that the tattwas have been created.

The other known characteristics of these five tattwas are *shabda* (sound), *varna* (colour) and *roopa* (form), which are created by the movement of energy within the tattwas. The different colours of the tattwas indicate the vibrational frequency of energy in each tattwa. As there is practically no vibration in akasha tattwa, it is black in colour. Vayu vibrates at the frequency of blue light, agni at the frequency of red light, apas as white light, and prithvi as yellow light.

The other manifestation of energy, which is sound, is characterized by the bija mantra of the tattwas. The bija mantra for akasha is *Ham*; vayu is *Yam*; agni *Ram*; apas *Vam*; and prithvi *Lam*. Sound and light together combine to give form to energy and, therefore, akasha is perceived in a circular form; vayu, as a hexagon; agni as an inverted triangle; apas as a crescent moon, and prithvi as a yellow square.

Recent research in cymatics has shown that light, sound and form are different stages in the manifestation of energy. In order to verify this, a mantra was correctly uttered into a tonometer, which reproduced the mantra in its visual form. The tattwa mantras have corresponding forms and colours, and one can be substituted for the other, as a base for meditation.

What happens after death

These tattwas exist on the collective or universal realm, as well as the individual realm. The cosmic realm is where creation is being eternally enacted and the individual realm is where the tattwas are entrapped in matter. When matter decays or disintegrates, these individual tattwas return to the universal realm and mix with their respective cosmic counterparts. At the time of death, the individual tattwas that compose the body and mind return to their source. Thus, akasha returns to akasha, vayu to vayu, agni to agni, apas to apas, prithvi to prithvi, awaiting creation into other forms of matter.

Finally, in an analysis of the tattwas, it is important to specify that these tattwas enact their role only at the behest of the 'principle of intelligence' i.e. consciousness. Without consciousness, these tattwas are immobile and dormant.

9

The Individual Tattwas

Akasha tattwa: the ether element

The word *akasha* signifies that which provides the space for matter to become existent. On a gross level it can be defined as the distance between two objects. It also refers to ether. Akasha, which is the subtlest of the panchatattwas, is all-pervading and motionless.

Akasha tattwa is responsible for the entire range of gross, subtle and causal sound perception conveyed through the sense organ *srotra* or ear. We know that sound requires a medium through which it can travel. No sound can travel in a vacuum, so akasha tattwa is considered to be the conveyor of sound.

The vibration of this tattwa is said to be so subtle that it cannot be perceived by the external senses. Our senses have not been tuned to that frequency, therefore, as long as we function through them, we cannot experience the subtle vibration of akasha or ether. It is said that ether travels faster than the speed of light, which has the highest velocity known to man.

Light originates from a point and travels from that point in a particular direction. A ray of light emanating from a source cannot travel in more than one direction. The quality of akasha, however, is space giving and its movement is diffused in many directions. So when the mental frequencies correlate to that of akasha through dhyana, one's experiences can transgress beyond time. One can then perceive the past, present and future.

Akasha tattwa is limitless and pervades the entire cosmos, therefore, its form is perceived as a circular void. As void exists in the absence of light, akasha has been described as transparent or black, bearing no colour. Within blackness, however, all the colours of the spectrum are contained. Thus, the yantra of akasha tattwa visualized in tattwa shuddhi is a circular black void dotted with many colours.

Akasha tattwa is not material in the ordinary sense. Thus it has not been possible to discover ether by physical means. However, it has been possible for the tattwa jnanis, who have transcended the gross mind, to realize the essence of akasha tattwa. That is why tantra has termed this tattwa as mental and not physical in nature, and as 'the space of the consciousness' in front of the closed eyes, known as *chidakasha*.

Akasha tattwa is responsible for creating the idea of space and in the human body, it controls the space surrounding the different organs. At the level of mind, akasha tattwa controls the emotions and passions in man. It can be said that when akasha tattwa is predominant, the mind is turned away from the sensorial experiences with which we are familiar. However, this occurs very rarely as the flow of akasha is only for five minutes in each hour. With this in view, it is no wonder that the majority of people remain in the realm of sensorial experiences. It is only the tattwa jnani who can transcend this by inducing the flow of akasha tattwa.

Akasha tattwa is most influential for spiritual progress. In terms of bondage to material gain, it can be called a destructive element, but for spiritual progress it is the most influential. So it is advisable that when akasha tattwa is flowing, one should practise concentration and meditation.

Physically, akasha is located at the top of the head. Mentally, it is related to the unconscious mind. Its psychic location is in vishuddhi chakra. The spiritual experiences it awakens are related to *jana loka* and *anandamaya kosha*, the causal body and beyond.

Vayu tattwa: the air element

Vayu has been translated as air, or anything in the gaseous form, and has the nature of wind. When the dark void of akasha tattwa is disturbed by motion, light energy is created. This reduces the blackness of the void and gives rise to the grey-blue colour which is distinctive of vayu tattwa. Thus the yantra of vayu visualized in tattwa shuddhi is of six grey-blue gaseous dots, forming a hexagon.

Vayu tattwa stands for kinetic energy in all its diverse forms: electrical, chemical and even vital. In this sense it even includes the prana in the body. The innate quality of vayu is movement through contraction and expansion, and it controls these qualities in the body through the five vital airs: prana, apana, samana, udana, vyana.

In the physical body, vayu tattwa enables the sensation of touch to be conveyed through the sense organ *twacha* or skin, via the sensory nerves, to their corresponding centre in the brain. The sense of touch is the most general function of vayu tattwa. However, if this sense is developed and made supersensitive, we could respond to sensations of much higher frequency, such as the movement of pure energy within and without us.

Vayu tattwa, like its cause, akasha tattwa, is invisible in the material sense. At this subtle stage, matter is still in its undifferentiated form. It can be described as energy in motion. Constant motion creates change and, therefore, the influence of vayu tattwa causes instability and fickleness in a person and the environment.

Due to its destabilizing influence, vayu can also be harmful for material gains. However, it is beneficial for literary pursuits because the flow of vayu tattwa influences the thought processes which are responsible for the unexpected 'brain wave'. For example, if you sit down to write a book during the flow of vayu tattwa, it is likely to be a best seller!

Physically, vayu tattwa is situated in the region from the heart to the eyebrows. Mentally, it is related to the subconscious mind. Psychically it is located in anahata chakra. The spiritual experiences related to this tattwa correspond to *maha loka* and *vijnanamaya kosha* or the intuitive body.

Agni tattwa: the fire element

Agni or fire is also known as *tejas*, which means 'to sharpen' or 'to whet'. This tattwa is energy in its first stage of manifestation, when it is primarily conceived as light. It is by the appearance of light that form is perceived. In the absence of light there is no form which can be perceived. Thus agni represents that quality which gives definition or form to the different kinds of energy in vayu tattwa, from which it has evolved. Agni tattwa is responsible for the perception of form or roopa, which is cognized through the sense organ of *chakshu* or eye.

The birth of form is closely connected with the birth of ego. We know that ego identifies with form, which results in attachment. Therefore, without the presence of form there can be no attachment. So we have to understand agni tattwa, not just as the first manifestation of form, but also as the stage when ahamkara begins to assert itself. As light lends form to energy, the ahamkara, which has been developing simultaneously, becomes aware of something outside itself for the first time. Thus the germ of individual ego is born.

Light is energy vibration at different frequencies and these can be perceived as various colours. Therefore, the colours representing the tattwas denote the vibrational frequency of that particular tattwa. In agni tattwa, energy vibrates at the frequency of red light, which is indicative of fire or excessive heat. Thus the yantra of agni in tattwa shuddhi is a fiery red triangle.

Agni tattwa has often been termed as a devouring force and is known to represent instability. Even in the world around us, we see that fire consumes anything that it meets, changing its shape, colour and perhaps destiny. In this sense, the influence of fire can be called destructive, but viewed in a more philosophical light, it can be seen as a catalyst for change, growth and evolution.

67

At this stage of evolution, the vibration of energy, which is responsible for radiation and heat, is increased. This increase in vibration causes the particles of agni tattwa to move incessantly and thus spread itself. Therefore, agni tattwa is said to contain the quality to increase as well as to consume.

In the physical body, agni tattwa regulates the fire of digestion, appetite, thirst and sleep, and it either increases or destroys them. Therefore, agni tattwa has to be controlled, and that is why in the yogic texts it is advised to 'fan the fire' of digestion through tantric and yogic practices.

Due to the restructuring quality of agni tattwa, it cannot merely be termed as an element of destruction, because through the destruction there is creation. For example, fire is used for destroying the impurities in metal ores and extracting the pure essence of gold, silver and so on. In daily life, the influence of agni tattwa can lead to 'hot situations' such as arguments, quarrels, accidents or even environmental catastrophes, which invariably bring change and growth.

Physically, agni tattwa is located in the region between the heart and the navel. Mentally, it is related to the subconscious mind. Its psychic location is in manipura chakra. The spiritual experiences related to this tattwa belong to the dimension of *swar loka* and *manomaya kosha*, the mental body.

Apas tattwa: the water element

Apas or water is derived from the root *aap*, which means 'to pervade'. Apas tattwa can be described as a vast quantity of intensely active matter which has begun to emerge out of agni tattwa. It is matter that has not yet been broken up into cohesive and separate bodies, because the atoms and molecules reverberating within this tattwa are still in a state of chaos. It is said that the physical universe is arranging itself in apas tattwa before its emergence. Hence the term 'pregnant waters' alluding to the idea of the universe contained within the womb of apas.

However, the movement and activity within the matter emerging out of apas tattwa is almost imperceptible, as the

Prithvi लं

Apas वं

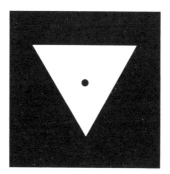

Agni रं

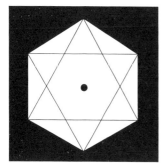

Vayu यं

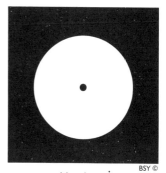

Akasha हं

BSY ©

atoms at this stage are confined to less space. For example, the atoms of hydrogen and oxygen combined in water do not have the same freedom of movement as they do in vapour. Similarly, the atoms of apas tattwa do not have the freedom of movement as in agni, vayu or akasha tattwa. Thus it is perceived, not as turbulence, but as a placid ocean of water, and the apas tattwa yantra visualized in tattwa shuddhi is that of a white crescent moon encircled by water.

In the physical body also, apas is the first tangible tattwa to emerge as matter, in the form of blood, mucus, bile, lymphatic fluid and so on. Thus it is known to control the fluids in the body.

As apas contains within it matter about to be created, it is considered to have a more creative influence on worldly events than akasha, agni or vayu. However, as the matter within apas tattwa is continually altering itself into newer arrangements, the beneficial results occurring when apas tattwa is active are not permanent. This tattwa also influences thoughts related to oneself and worldly affairs.

Physically, apas tattwa is located in the region between the navel and the knees. Mentally, it is related to the subconscious and conscious mind. Its psychic location is in swadhisthana chakra. The spiritual experiences related to this tattwa correspond with *bhuvar loka* and the *pranamaya kosha* or vital body.

Prithvi tattwa: the earth element

The last tattwa in the matter/energy complex is *prithvi* or earth. Prithvi is also known as *bhumi*, which means 'to be' or 'to exist'. It also means the ground and earth we live upon, which signifies existence. In prithvi tattwa, the particles of energy have been condensed until they appear almost static, rotating only within the immediate space surrounding each atom. Thus, in this tattwa, energy appears as concrete matter, in its solid, liquid or gaseous forms.

In prithvi tattwa, energy vibrates at a much lower frequency than in the preceding tattwas and can be perceived as yellow light. Therefore, in tattwa shuddhi the yantra of prithvi tattwa is visualized as a yellow square.

Prithvi tattwa is attributed with the qualities of solidity, weight and cohesion. In the physical body it is the solidity in the cellular structure of bones and other organs, and creates weight and density. Prithvi, having evolved out of the preceding tattwas, also contains their qualities, however, smell is its predominating quality. The subtle perception of prithvi is *gandha* or smell, which is conveyed through the sense organ of the nose.

As opposed to vayu tattwa, prithvi tattwa brings stability and permanence in every respect, physically, mentally and in the environment. It is most conducive for material profit and the pursuit of worldly ventures.

Physically, prithvi tattwa is located in the region between the toes and the knees. Mentally, it is related to the conscious and subconscious levels of mind. Its psychic location is in mooladhara chakra. The spiritual experiences related to this tattwa correspond with the dimensions of *bhu loka* and *annamaya kosha*, the gross body.

10

Tattwas and Koshas

The different levels of existence in which the five tattwas or mahabhutas manifest, are known as koshas in yoga. *Kosha* literally means 'sheath' or 'covering', and in this context refers to the different layers covering the inner essence of man, that is the spirit or pure consciousness. Man is said to be enveloped in five such koshas, each more subtle in vibration than the preceding one, and each related to a particular level of awareness and experience.

The first and grossest covering is annamaya kosha, the sheath made of food; next, pranamaya kosha, the sheath made of prana; then manomaya kosha, the sheath made of mind and thought; vijnanamaya kosha, the sheath made of intuition; and lastly anandamaya kosha, the sheath composed of bliss.

Annamaya kosha is related to the conscious mind and physical body. Manomaya kosha is related to the subconscious mind and subtle body; pranamaya kosha is the link between the two, relating to both states of mind and body. Anandamaya kosha relates to the unconscious mind and causal body, leading to transcendental consciousness. Vijnanamaya kosha is the link between subconscious mind/subtle body and unconscious mind/causal body. Annamaya kosha is predominantly influenced by prithvi tattwa, pranamaya by apas, manomaya by agni, vijnanamaya by vayu and anandamaya by akasha.

The subtle dimensions of man's existence can only be reached through the practices of tantra, yoga and other spiritual practices. In tattwa shuddhi sadhana, you are influencing annamaya and pranamaya koshas by controlling the breath and increasing the pranic supply. Manomaya and pranamaya koshas are influenced by concentration. Vijnanamaya kosha is awakened by trataka on the tattwa yantras. The influence on these four koshas leads to an experience in anandamaya kosha. However, there is no direct practice to affect anandamaya kosha.

These experiences, which arise in the form of colours, lights, smells and so on due to the practice of tattwa shuddhi, are a product of these invisible bodies. The deeper you travel into the subtle and causal bodies, the greater the experience becomes because the tattwas are a part and parcel of every cell and atom in the body. Thus tattwa shuddhi sadhana enables you to travel deeper into the recesses of the subtler layers which compose the human aura.

Loka	Plane	Predominant Tattwa
Bhu	physical plane	prithvi (earth)
Bhuvar	intermediate plane	apas (water)
Swar	divine plane	agni (fire)
Maha	plane of saints and siddhas	vayu (air)
Jana	plane of rishis and munis	akasha (ether)
Tapo	plane of liberated souls	mahat (higher consciousness)
Satya	plane of ultimate truth	shiva/shakti (consciousness/energy)

The seven lokas: realms of consciousness

The invisible bodies or koshas are also linked and related to the seven planes of consciousness and existence. These planes are known as *lokas*. Each loka is a plane of existence through which the consciousness is evolving, as it slowly becomes free from the matter in which it is embedded.

The influence of the tattwas pervades each of these lokas, except the last, satya loka, which is beyond the influence of the panchatattwas or mahabhutas. It is important to realize that through tattwa shuddhi sadhana we increase the awareness and purify the tattwas in all dimensions of existence.

11

Tattwas and the Breath

In the *Chandogyopanishad* it is stated that the five tattwas evolved from the mind, mind from prana and prana from pure consciousness. Thus the tattwas are present in every form of creation. In the physical body they are manifest as chitta shakti, prana shakti and atma shakti, which act on the body and mind through energy channels or nadis and the breath or swara.

Swara means 'flow' or 'movement'. *Nadi* also means 'flow'. Nadi is the flow of shakti in the subtle body, and swara is the flow of shakti in the breath. Therefore, the swara shastras deal with the science of the flow of breath and nadis.

The three shaktis flowing in the breath are channelled through three main nadis in the body, known as ida, pingala and sushumna. It is said that, within the physical framework of the body, there is a network of 72,000 nadis. All these carry prana or vital energy throughout the entire body, but out of them the three nadis, ida, pingala and sushumna have a major influence on the psychophysical and spiritual states of the body, mind and consciousness.

Chitta shakti, or the force of ida, is the vital mental energy which governs all the functions of thought, mind and chitta. All mental activity is a result of the flow and dominance of ida. This flow of energy is connected to the flow of breath through the left nostril, which is known to influence right brain hemisphere activities. It is also known

75

as *chandra* (moon) *swara* and considered as the negative polarity of energy within the body.

Prana shakti, which flows in pingala, is the vital life force and positive polarity of energy which governs all active physical functions. The physical work you perform throughout the day is a direct consequence of the level of prana shakti that is flowing in you. The activities of pingala are connected to the flow of breath through the right nostril, which influences left brain hemisphere activities. It is also known as *surya* (sun) *swara*.

The third shakti or energy, atma shakti, is channelled through sushumna nadi, the central passage of prana. Whereas ida is the channel of the mental energy force and pingala is the channel for the vital energy force, sushumna is the channel for the spiritual energy force. Sushumna is a neutral energy and when it is active, the breath flows through both nostrils simultaneously. Then the flow of both ida and pingala are harmonized, and this occurrence is known to influence the activities of the higher dormant brain centres.

In the physical body, these three nadis correspond to the parasympathetic (ida), sympathetic (pingala) and autonomic (sushumna) nervous systems. However, throughout the life of most people, sushumna remains dormant. Until sushumna is awakened through the practices of tantra, yoga or other spiritual practices, an individual is entirely under the control of chitta and prana shakti, ida/pingala.

These three aspects of energy manifest in the physical breath or swaras in a cyclical pattern. The flow of ida or the chandra swara lasts for approximately one hour, after which it changes to pingala for the next hour and then back to ida.

At the time of changeover, there is a brief span of a few seconds when the third nadi, sushumna, flows. This cycle continues day and night and is strongly influenced by the lunar/solar movements, adjusting itself to the bright and dark fortnights of the lunar cycle.

As the entire body and mind structure is made up of the five tattwas, they are inherent in every aspect of our existence and can even be witnessed in the flow of the swara. Each tattwa has a particular pranic frequency and affects the various body mechanisms. The activities of the tattwas cause the breath or swara to flow in different directions, for varying distances and durations, and influence the triune energy system of ida, pingala, and sushumna.

The two nadis, ida/pingala, channel shakti or energy into the various chakras or energy centres situated in the spinal column, beginning from mooladhara, right up to ajna chakra. These centres increase in vibration and are intersected by ida/pingala. The influence of the tattwas is also conveyed to the chakras through the swara. Each chakra is dominated by one of the five elements, mooladhara by the earth element (the lowest vibration of prana), swadhisthana by water, manipura by fire, and anahata by air. The subtlest element, ether, rules over vishuddhi chakra, the throat centre, and the chakras beyond vishuddhi fall under the influence of the subtler elements of the antah karana.

Just as the different swaras influence and govern different spheres of mental, physical and spiritual experience, the five tattwas also have individual characteristics which affect our state of mind, body and consciousness. For example, when prithvi or earth element is active, one's thoughts relate to material gain, whereas if ether is flowing then there are no thoughts, but complete stillness or shoonya. Therefore, to understand the levels of awareness we are experiencing, we have not only to know which tattwa is active, but also which swara is flowing at that time. In the final analysis, it is a combination of both the swara and predominating tattwa which influence our physical, psychological and transcendental states of mind.

It is said in the *Shiva Swarodaya* that if the element of fire is predominant during the flow of sushumna, it consumes the fruit of all actions. This is because when sushumna flows, the awareness is absorbed in the subtlest tattwa, *paramtattwa*, which is beyond action and result. Agni tattwa, in combination with sushumna, intensifies this effect. This is why it is said that when sushumna begins to flow, one should stop all work and sit down for meditation or spiritual practices.

If the element of ether is active during the flow of sushumna, then the mind travels at a very great speed; like a swift rocket it is catapulted into higher experience. At that time it is easy to transcend material or external awareness, and meditation during that period will undoubtedly give good results. However, this combination is known to occur very rarely.

During the flow of ida and pingala, these five tattwas arise separately in succession. In each hour of the chandra and surya swaras, all five tattwas are active individually in the order of air, fire, earth, water and ether respectively. Each tattwa has a fixed duration during which it flows, and when that is over it is replaced by the next tattwa. It is possible to detect the prevailing tattwa in the swara at any particular time in several ways.

A tattwa yogi, who has complete knowledge or jnana of the tattwas in relation to the swara, can judge his physical, mental, emotional and spiritual state and act in accordance with that. However, more important than this is knowing how to induce the experience of your true nature through awareness of the tattwas in the different swaras.

How to recognize the tattwas from the breath

These tattwas have individual colours, forms, tastes, locations, directions, durations, sequence and distance of flow in the breath, as presented in the following table.

A tattwa yogi can define the active tattwa that is flowing, by examining the nature of the perceptions arising therefrom. After developing proficiency in the art of defining the tattwa, he develops the experience of the tattwas through several tantric practices that accentuate their flow.

One of these practices is trataka on the tattwa yantras. The yantras can be inscribed on metal or drawn on paper with their respective mantras and appropriate colours. Then one performs trataka on each yantra for a number of days,

Characteristic	Prithvi	Apas	Agni	Vayu	Akasha
Colour	yellow	white	red	grey-blue	blackish
Form	square	crescent moon	inverted triangle	hexagon	circular
Taste	sweet	astringent	bitter	acidic/sour	pungent
Direction of breath flow	central	downward	upward	slanting	diffused
Duration	20 mins	16 mins	12 mins	8 mins	4 mins
Sequence	3rd	4th	2nd	1st	5th
Length of breath*	12	16	4	8	—

*Distance in fingers width from nostrils

mentally repeating its corresponding bija mantra. Beginning with the prithvi element, first develop proficiency in one yantra, before going onto the next. At the end of each practice, examine the flow of the tattwas by gazing into chidakasha, the space in front of the closed eyes (chidakasha dharana) and witnessing the forms and colours which arise.

As the tattwas are intimately connected with the tanmatras or sense perceptions, one can even experience the senses in their subtle form. This should also be observed as it is a vital indication. For example, one may hear inner sounds, smell fragrances, taste different things, or feel the touch of something against the skin without an external cause.

Other practices which are useful for witnessing the tattwas are *naumukhi mudra* (closing of the nine gates) and *yoni mudra* or *shanmukhi mudra* (closing of the seven gates).While performing these, you should analyze the colours and forms which appear in front of your closed eyes. The active tattwa can also be detected by breathing out through the nose onto a mirror and observing the shape of the vapour made by the breath.

Chhayopasana, i.e. trataka on one's shadow, is another tantric practice which is very powerful for determining the flow of the tattwa. However, this practice requires expert knowledge and the shastras recommend the guidance of a guru in order to perfect it.

These and several other practices help to develop our knowledge and experience of the tattwas in action. They are the scientific methods of closing the doors to the outer perceptions, and opening the ones to the inner perceptions of colours, sounds, smells and so on.

12

Mantra, Yantra and Mandala

Intricately woven into the theory and philosophy of tantra is the science of mantra, yantra and mandala. Tantra is both a philosophy and a practical science, and its sublime theories become efficacious through the use of mantra, yantra and mandala. We are often assailed by systems and philosophies which talk about transformation of an individual and attainment of higher knowledge and intuition. They talk about moral and ethical disciplines, which are undoubtedly ideal qualities, but few people can even hope to attain them. Intellectual acceptance is not enough to transform an individual. After all, a philosophy without any guidelines for practical application is mere intellectualism.

Tantra's unique quality is that it does not proclaim high-sounding or abstract philosophies without substantiating them through a systematic and thorough explanation of their practical and daily application. This it has achieved through the highly evolved science of mantra, yantra and mandala. In order to fully understand the mechanics of these three basic tools of tantra which are utilized in all tantric sadhana, including tattwa shuddhi, it is necessary to understand each one of them.

Mandala

First of all, let us examine the mandala from which arose the rich art of tantric iconography, temples, art, architecture and music. Any form which is pictorially or visually created within the consciousness of man forms a mandala. In order to create a mandala, you have to be able to see within yourself, not in the form of thought, but in the form of vision, as clearly as you see the world with open eyes. The clearer your inner vision, the more accurate and powerful is the mandala you create.

The principle of a mandala is that it lives within a circle, thus any mandala that is visualized has to be represented within the symmetry of a circle. This is due to the fact that the circle is considered a primal form, and it is curious that even the earth on which we live is not flat but round or elliptical. The formation of a mandala follows the same principle as that of light as expounded by scientific theory. Light waves move in a curve, thus bending space and forming an arc or curvature. The circular aura is an essential factor of the mandala and this is clearly evident in all the ancient tantric mandalas existing today.

Anything can form a mandala: a tree, a house, a car, an animal, a human being; even your body is a mandala. When you are able to visualize through the inner eye, the form you see of a tree or any other object is very precise, even more precise than what you see with your eyes open. You may be visualizing the same object both inside and outside, but the difference is that when you visualize an object through the higher mind, you momentarily catch a glimpse of what lies behind the form. Thus you are able to perceive more than the average eye.

After all, each one of us can see a tree, a house, an animal or a beautiful landscape and then reproduce it on canvas or paper. However that is an insufficient mandala because we have not been able to see beyond the object; we have not perceived the object on a linear dimension, or in the form of colour or sound. Therefore, it cannot convey to us any meaning beyond the fact that it is what it is meant to be.

In order to create a mandala that has both power and force, both inner clarity and the ability to replicate the inner vision is important. Some people can clearly see inside, but they cannot recreate externally what they have seen. This is what often distinguishes a good artist from a bad one. Both may have the same inner vision, but it differs in clarity and reproduction. Therefore, a mandala is the essence of an object perceived by one who has refined his inner vision; an inner cosmic picture, which is reproduced for all to see.

The mandala you create is dependent on your level of consciousness. The more evolved your consciousness is, the more universal will be the mandala you create. A universal mandala is that which is created through a mind in tune with the cosmic consciousness. Therefore, it is applicable and relevant to all mankind, whereas the mandalas which are created by minds that are still on the individual plane have less universal appeal and less ability to invoke higher levels of consciousness in others. Moreover, certain mandalas are created by those who have transcended the material plane and become enraptured in supraconscious ecstasy. It is these mandalas which can evoke spiritual experience in others, and it is primarily these that tantra has employed.

Every culture and civilization has its mandalas to offer us, and the quality of the creations gives us a clear idea of the level of consciousness of that society. All forms of art, sculpture and architecture are mandala creations which have been envisaged in the abyss of the mind and then recreated. That is why the work is so profound, has so much depth and can influence so many generations of people, so many centuries later, to stand awed and struck dumb.

The difference between a mandala created by an artist and that created by a mystic is significant. An artist communicates his inner experience by translating it into a concept that is bound by time and space, because his inside is not as profound as that of a mystic. It often only conveys his emotions but not a metaphysical truth. A mystic, on the other hand, goes far beyond the limitations of the finite mind, emotions and intellect and, therefore, his experiences relate more profoundly to the universal concepts of the cosmos. Both artist and mystic explore and depict inner truths. However, an artist expels the experiences through his work of art, whereas the mystic continues to develop one experience into another. A mystic is not aiming to discover inner visions, but that which is even beyond. If an artist were to do the same, he would be transformed into a mystic. Therefore, all art based on divine inner experience has been able to withstand the test of time, and exists as an immortal and eternal idea.

It is significant that, in India, all forms of art, music and architecture are deeply influenced by the spiritual insight of its ancestral past. Classical Indian music, through its blend of melody, beat and rhythm, creates a mandala that can evoke a response in the deepest layers of consciousness. The artwork of Ajanta and Ellora caves, the famed Khajuraho temples, the Konarak sun temple in Orissa, and millions of other such works, are in actual fact mandalas that deeply influence the consciousness of those who see them.

The influence on the consciousness is always very subtle, albeit very precise. You cannot know the levels of mind that the consciousness explores and influences. It is the subconscious and unconscious mind with which the mandalas converse and, therefore, they are able to awaken inner visions. It is through this process that the deeper layers of the mind begin to manifest.

In tantra, mandalas have also been depicted as pictorial representations of divine forces, symbolized as theriomorphic and anthropomorphic forms. Tantra asserts that these forms of divinity do not exist as objective entities anywhere in any part of the stratospheres, presiding over our destinies. However, it does feel the necessity of developing the idea of divinity in human form in order to make it comprehensible to the gross awareness of man.

Tantra asks how a person who is incapable of seeing within can visualize or experience formless reality. We cannot even experience or witness our own thoughts, let alone higher reality. So the mandala forms of devis and devas developed

84

into elaborate and visually arresting symbols. However, the grosser imagination of divinity is ultimately to be transcended and developed into the experience of formless reality.

This mandala symbology of devis and devas covers an infinite array of forms, colours and depictions. Some are ravishingly beautiful, others provocative; some kind and compassionate, others grotesque and fearful; some suggest divine powers and others material gain. In each case the structure is elaborately detailed and designed to evoke a corresponding response within the consciousness of the aspirant. This symbology is based on the eternal archetypal structure of man's collective unconscious and these mandalas draw out those archetypes as a magnet draws out iron filings from a heap of diamonds.

Concentration on a mandala awakens the deep-seated samskaras within you and reveals the unknown mysteries in the form of dreams, visions and mental action. You are not compelled to face the samskaras directly and so they do not affect your action in daily life. They are dispensed with during meditation and dream. It is a way of bypassing a terrible and fearsome enemy for which you have no defence. These mandalas, which are always very aesthetic and visually arresting, are able to capture and direct the imagination, which is the subtle link to the higher mind.

Perhaps the most controversial mandala which tantra has defined to date is the kriya of *maithuna*. The kriya of maithuna forms a mandala that has corresponding yantras and mantras. The erotic sculptures of the Khajuraho temples, and other temples in Orissa, are based entirely on the tantric belief that maithuna is an act through which the divine powers can be invoked. Man represents shiva or the positive polarity and woman represents shakti or the negative polarity. Through their exoteric and esoteric union, they create a field of power or an energy circuit, which is the mandala. These works do not denote the carnal passions, but union on the highest esoteric level, which is parallel to the union of energy and consciousness, shiva and shakti.

The linga and yoni mandala is also symbolic of this higher union, and that is why this symbol has been venerated in India for centuries. Linga signifies that which is effulgent, and yoni signifies the source. Therefore, linga should be understood as the symbol of pure consciousness and yoni as the source of energy, which together are the forces behind creation. Man and woman unite on the physical plane to relive the experience of unity from which they have evolved. This unity is an internal experience, just as a spiritual experience is an internal experience.

Tantra is perhaps the only philosophy that has been bold enough to say this. Others have either remained quiet about it, or exploited the idea by branding it as a sin, and thereby inducing a sense of guilt and depravity in man for doing it. However, guilt and shame are very hard to expel from the consciousness. They stay with man a long time, controlling his actions, mind, personality and life. Unless man is able to break through these barriers, he cannot attain the higher experience. For that experience he will have to eradicate his guilt and shame.

The idea of sin was cleverly planted in the minds of people by certain philosophical sects because, for them, religion had become a power game, and in order to enforce power, you need the support of the masses. So they decided to give the masses a cancerous dose of guilt and shame, which in time would spread its tentacles and manifest in every part of the body, mind, chitta, ego, and intellect, thus keeping him forever enslaved.

However, the tantrics did not care for external power because they had realized the power within. They did not care for the masses, but only for a chosen few who were courageous and valiant enough to face up to the real inner experience. Today maithuna may have degenerated into a mere exoteric act due to the strong repressions and admonitions imposed by certain religions. However, tantra says maithuna is not a sin, but an act of worship which can help the individual transcend the lower consciousness, a concept which most people disbelieve due to their complex of guilt and shame. Thus this knowledge was kept secret and only handed down from guru to disciple, which established the tradition of an eternal mandala, because the guru and disciple tradition begins and ends at the same point, which signifies that it continues forever.

When examined carefully it is evident that the practice of tattwa shuddhi is also skilfully arranged as a mandala. We begin the practice at some point of evolution and travel very far into the self. After having followed the process of evolution and involution of creation, we find ourselves back at the same point, as if it were an endless circle that we had been following from birth to death to birth. When you see the reality behind your birth and existence, the desire for liberation awakens, compelling you to discover the means to free yourself from this endless cycle of cause and event.

This circular form given to the practice of tattwa shuddhi is no coincidence. It has a deliberate pattern, a deliberate idea, a deliberate force, and that force is the secret power of the mandala, which you can only know when you pursue it, as a young man pursues his first love. The practice gives you a momentary glance into that secret power; just a flash of the eye and the experience is gone, so that often you may not even know you had it. However, the effect can be felt in the subtler dimension of your consciousness, and it is that part of you that tantra is trying to reach.

Yantra

Just as the mandala is a pictorial representation of an inner vision, so the yantra is an abstract mathematical representation of the inner vision. As the awareness penetrates deeper levels of consciousness, the inner experiences also change. They become more abstract and universal, as seen in nature. Nature is not the trees, rivers, oceans and sky as we see them. That is the gross form. But behind the gross form, there is an abstract subtle form and it is this form that the yantra represents. Every image has a corresponding yantra that is defined by the linear dimension. In fact, everything in nature can be experienced in its original form, the yantra.

Just as all forms of creation or matter are nothing but energy, so a yantra also contains inherent energy. Due to its mathematical precision, it is a powerhouse of energy, and by visualization and concentration on a yantra, you can induce the awakening of the equivalent energy within you.

A yantra creates a field of power that lives, breathes and moves with life, and within which the powers of the divine can be invoked. In order to perceive this, you will have to develop a new way of seeing, by sharpening the innate faculty in which the corresponding images are stored. These images do exist within you and are as much a part of you as your anger, greed and passions.

A yantra is composed of a combination of the basic primordial shapes, i.e. a bindu or point, a circle, a square and a triangle. The focal point of a yantra is always at the centre, or bindu. Bindu is the point or nucleus representing the seed from which creation has evolved and into which it will return, i.e. the process of creation and dissolution. It also represents the union of the two dual principles of the universe, shiva and shakti, consciousness and energy. Bindu represents the state of their union preceding creation. It is also represented in the physical body as the nucleus or centre called *bindu visarga*, which is located at the top back portion of the head. In meditation, the aspirant uses the external bindu of the yantra as a focal point of concentration, in order to experience the contraction of time/space within the bindu of the physical body.

Space cannot be defined by less than three lines, so the triangle is considered to be the first form to emerge out of creation. This triangle is known as *moola trikona* or the root triangle. In its inverted form, the triangle represents the root matrix of creation or prakriti and the upward pointing triangle represents purusha or consciousness. We often find in a yantra an intersection of an inverted and upward-pointing triangle representing both consciousness and energy.

The circle represents the cycle of timelessness, where there is no beginning and no end, only eternity, and implies the process of birth, life and death as an eternal cycle of events. The square is the substratum on which the yantra rests and denotes the physical or terrestrial world which has ultimately to be transcended.

The whole visual concept of the yantra, although symbolic, has vast significance in terms of the spiritual evolution and experience of man. It forms a pathway from the outer physical experience to the innermost chambers of man's creation and existence. This is done so subtly and systematically that one can never grasp its true significance through the limitations of the conscious mind. Nevertheless, these subtle manipulations are taking place, consciously or otherwise.

It has been observed that the intelligence quotient, intuitive response and mental awareness of children who have been exposed to yantras and mandalas, with no conscious attention drawn to them, have shown a remarkable improvement. The yantra influences our creative and intuitive intelligence, however, its true significance is the flowering of the spiritual experience. Slowly, but gradually and systematically, the yantra leads to the unfoldment of the multiplicity of layers which comprise our whole being. In tattwa shuddhi sadhana, the yantras we create are of the four primal forms described above.

Mantra

Just as every thought has a corresponding image or form, so every image or form has a corresponding nada, vibration or sound. These sounds are known as mantras. *Mantra* literally means 'contemplation upon that which leads to liberation'. A tall claim no doubt, and one may well be sceptical at the possibilities of a sound leading to liberation.

However, we have underestimated the power of sound. We know that sound has the capacity to shatter glass or even start an avalanche. We know a little about the influence of sound on the human brain and body as well as on animals and even plants. So we can definitely accept that sound influences us on certain levels. Nevertheless, when we are confronted with the idea that sound can lead to *moksha* or liberation, we say, "No, that is impossible!"

In fact, we have already seen that nada is one of the first manifest forms of creation. Even the Bible begins with the statement, "In the beginning was the word." In Indian philosophy, this 'word' is known as Om, which is the eternal nada or cosmic mantra. In the *Mandukyopanishad* there is a very clear explanation of the mantra Om and how it stimulates and expands the different levels of consciousness. The mantra Om is made up of three sounds 'A', 'U' and 'M', and each of these sounds vibrates at a different frequency. These different frequencies influence the consciousness in different ways. When you are repeating the mantra Om, you are actually raising your consciousness to the frequency of that mantra. This is true for all mantras.

Nada has four frequencies: *para* (cosmic), *pashyanti* (causal), *madhyama* (subtle) and *vaikhari* (gross). These correspond to the four frequency levels of Om (conscious, subconscious, unconscious and transcendental or turiya state), depending on the level of frequency attained through chanting. Most aspirants remain in the vaikhari or madhyama stages and thus the level of experience is not even remotely close to liberation.

The entire Sanskrit language is composed of mantras. In Sanskrit the letters are not called letters, but are known as *akshara*, which means 'imperishable'. Each letter of the alphabet is a mantra and can be used as such. That is why the act of merely reading the Vedas in Sanskrit has been said to lead to liberation. The Sanskrit language is deeply related to the consciousness of man, and it is not just mere words which have been composed for the sake of communication.

The most powerful form of mantra is the bija mantra. *Bija* means seed and bija mantras are the root sounds from which all other mantras and sounds have arisen. Bija mantra is a force of concentrated energy which is ascribed to a particular level of consciousness. In tattwa shuddhi, the mantras we utilize are bija mantras related to the five tattwas. This is important because bija mantras affect the root cause of your being. It is no use trying to discover the meaning of these mantras. The only meaning a mantra can convey is metaphysical; it is sufficient to say that through the mantra you are conversing with your inner self and the cosmos.

It is even known in tantra that each part of the physical body has a corresponding mantra by which it is influenced. These mantras are used in the ceremony of nyasa to transform the physical body into a receptacle for the higher powers, which are awakened through tattwa shuddhi and other esoteric practices.

Not only does the physical body have its corresponding mantras, but the sound produced by the movement of the breath is also a mantra. This sound is known as *Soham* and *Hamso*. Together *So* and *Ham* are spontaneously repeated with each breath, 21,600 times, each day and night, throughout the life of an individual. Thus it is known as the *ajapa japa* mantra. In the Upanishads it is said that contemplating on this mantra alone is sufficient to arouse kundalini and higher awareness. In tattwa shuddhi we utilize this mantra at the very beginning to induce the feeling of identification with the universal consciousness.

Mantras are either cruel, benevolent or mixed. This depends on the character of the letters of which they are composed. For example, mantras in which the tattwa of fire or air are in excess are destructive, whereas mantras in which the earth and water tattwas are in abundance are benevolent. Mantras composed of the ether element are beneficial for spiritual achievement.

Mantras are inseparable from yantras. Every yantra has a corresponding mantra, through the repetition of which the yantra becomes efficacious. By repetition of the mantra at the higher levels of frequencies of nada, the consciousness is heightened, and through concentration on yantra, the consciousness is centralized or focalized to a point of explosion.

At one level of awareness, the inner experience is in the form of thought and emotion; at a higher level it becomes an inner pictorial vision or mandala. As you go deeper, it manifests as an abstract symbol or yantra, which later manifests as pure sound, nada or mantra. At every level of experience the energy is manifesting in different ways. The subtler the frequency of energy, the more profound the experience.

The mind also has to be understood as an energy force, not as a psychological creation. When the mind operates at a lower, grosser frequency of energy it becomes static, dull, inert or tamasic, but when you make subtle the frequency through mantra, yantra and mandala, it transcends the state of tamas, attaining a rajasic state and then the state of pure sattwa, which is mind at a very subtle frequency.

Concluding points about mantra, yantra and mandala

The tantric mantra, yantra and mandala are all a product of the profound inner vision of the yogis, rishis and seers, who have enquired deeply into the nature of the cosmos. They are a product of high states of spiritual enlightenment, ecstasy and experience. In that state of mind the consciousness transcends all barriers and, therefore, the experience is called universal.

As long as you are bound by time and space, your experiences are limited and related only to that dimension. However, when you transcend that, there is no religion, no caste, no creed and no sex, so how can the vision be limited? Moreover, in that state of mind you are one with the whole process of nature and can commune with her. Then all the visions become a part of the cosmic truth and those images follow the strict codes and laws which are inherent in every process of nature. This is evident in the tantric mantra, yantra and mandala which are all in perfect linear and geometrical harmony and balance.

In the tantric system, each mantra, yantra and mandala is calculated right down to the last detail. If it does not fulfil the exact mathematical equation which defines its balance, then it is inefficacious and incomplete. You need only to glance at some of these mandalas and yantras to verify their mathematical balance. In fact, that is one of the first aspects which attracts your attention.

In the tantric system, the mandala represents the visual iconographic form of a higher force, the yantra represents the abstract form of that force, and the mantra represents the subtle form. Thus each mandala has a corresponding yantra and mantra and one can be substituted for the other, according to the level of the aspirant, as they evoke the same results. However, different deities represent different levels of consciousness and are to be chosen on that basis.

In the practice of tattwa shuddhi, therefore, the yantras and mandalas that we create should be understood, not as religious, occult, mystic mysterious symbols, but as highly charged forces of energy which can evoke the same frequency within you to expand your consciousness.

13

Visualization and Imagination

One of the instrumental causes for the rapid progress of a tantric aspirant is due to the detailed process of inner visualization, which has been outlined in all tantric sadhana. This imaginative and creative inner visualization which tantra emphasizes is not chosen at random, but is deeply related to, and based on, the world of the psyche, which is a world of symbolism. As the mind explores the symbol it is led to ideas that lie beyond the grasp of reason, but which nevertheless have an indefinable link with one's structural past.

Today, due to the influence of western thinkers and philosophies, the world is more attuned to knowledge based on factual evidence or objective experience. However, there are a number of things beyond the range of human understanding which cannot be verified in a laboratory, but only through personal experience within the dark recesses of the mind. In spite of the subjectivity of this analysis, we are compelled to take note of it due to the transforming quality of those inner experiences.

In order to develop those inner visions, it is imperative that you unleash the creative imagination and visualizing capacities within you. Imagination is a dynamic process through which the thinker creates a dimension of experience, unattainable through a rational process of thinking. The wilder or more uninhibited the imagination is, the greater the range of experience.

Of course, we are all able to imagine in some form or other, but that is insufficient. Those imaginings are limited and do not transgress the boundaries of probability. They are restricted to the normal, social codes of behaviour and thought patterns. Moreover, they do not go beyond thought; they never become visions. If they did, we would all be visionaries or seers. A seer is one who can see within; one who has developed his imaginative faculty to such an extent that all knowledge is conveyed to him in the form of visual patterns. He is using the same faculty with which each one of us is endowed, but in a more dynamic and universal way.

Imagination, the source of creative power
It has been found that only those who have strong powers of imagination have the ability to create, because imagination is a mental force that can be utilized in any manner. As you build an inner world of visions and symbols, the forces of the mind become stronger because it is you who are creating those images through your own mental power, out of the vast potential that is dormant within you in the form of archetypes. Once the forces of the mind develop the power to imagine and create the train of thought that you wish to pursue, it spontaneously develops the power to achieve whatever it sets its eye upon.

In recent years, the process of inner visualization has been used very successfully for helping to treat cancer patients. The renowned Dr Ainslie Meares of Australia and Dr Simonton of America have both experimented with the idea of the patient visualizing an inner process of healing. The patient is led through a series of visualizations where the healthy cells and tissues attack the diseased ones, in much the same manner as one army attacks another. Much of the success depends on the capacity of the patient to concentrate, focus and visually imagine this process within himself. The results have indeed been rewarding.

Needless to say, the idea of treating cancer patients in this way has been derived from the emphasis laid on this aspect by tantra and yoga. In tantra, visualization and creative imagination act as a bridge between the objective and subjective worlds. Your imagination may focus on your objective experiences, but the images you create are purely subjective.

It is for this reason that tantra has developed the elaborate art of iconography. The icons act as a base from which the imagination of the aspirant is given a direction, a focus and a medium for concentration. Abstract imagination is undoubtedly more powerful, but very few can do it, at least in a creative manner, so that it achieves a beneficial result. Most people need guidance and direction at every step because the mind is untrained. It becomes distracted and dissipated easily or else it loses control. At times, this could be dangerous if your imagination is based on destruction. This is precisely why the disciplines of yoga become necessary, so that the mind spontaneously remains in the grip of the aspirant, no matter what heights he is scaling.

In order to use your imagination as a creative force, it is necessary to create a thought, visualize it, and maintain one-pointed concentration on it, until you have taken it to its point of culmination or exhaustion. Only then does the mind become powerful. However, the mind creates difficulties in the process and that is why the average person meets with disappointment and frustration.

In tattwa shuddhi, you are encouraged to explore within. You are given the opportunity to create colours, sounds, images and are asked to dwell on abstract ideas, visualizing them as concrete forms. You are introduced to both grotesque as well as pleasing images and although there are certain definite guidelines to help you, you are given the scope to venture as far as possible.

In the beginning, the images exist only in the form of thought, but gradually they develop into clearly defined pictures. This is only attained when the mind becomes more concentrated. As the mind dwells on these pictures which you yourself are creating, you are led to subtle experiences which otherwise remain unnoticed.

Imagination has to have a guideline

We have to pay heed to the process of imagination and visualization as a method of developing subtle and profound inner experiences, as well as a way of increasing the powers of the mind, not as a method of brainwashing, as many critics have conjectured. The symbols and images we use in the practice of tattwa shuddhi have been chosen due to their universality. They can be considered products of subjective experiences that have been verified objectively. They are the eternal archetypal symbols which can evoke profound spiritual experiences in man, no matter to which nationality or religion he belongs. They have been examined under the penetrating glare of those who have illumined their inner vision and are the only existing link between you and the eternal spirit which you are trying to grasp.

Tantric images often go beyond the boundaries of rationale. Some of the images have sixteen hands and three eyes, some are depicted naked and drinking blood, while others are shown carrying weapons of destruction. Kali is depicted with a garland of skulls, and Shiva is depicted with snakes crawling all over his body. Apart from their symbolical significance, these diverse illustrations are tantra's way of asserting that life can never be fitted into one mould, one idea and one way of thinking. To do that would simply be to denigrate the diversity of life. Rather, we have to experience life as variety and contradiction in order to be able to live it more fully.

In fact, today tantra stands as the only spiritual tradition which has kept this sphere of practical application alive and active, as a scientific treatment for the human mind and consciousness. Tantra believes that the imagination and inner experience should not be left to arbitrary moods which man experiences from time to time, rather, they should be inculcated under the command of his will. He should be competent to create a thought, develop and visualize it and then dispense with it. This is the basis for spiritual experience and also for any fulfilment you wish to have in your material life.

In order to do this, you will have to conform to the rules and injunctions laid down in the tantric practices. Tantra prescribes not only symbols and images to vitalize a desired idea, but also the way you should sit, how you should breathe, whether your room should be dark, and at which moment you should introduce a particular symbol. All this is to be done under the strict guidance of a master.

Image of Papa Purusha, the sinful man
The meditation practice done in tattwa shuddhi is full of unusual imagery, but the most bizarre is that of Papa Purusha, the sinful man, who symbolizes the cause of your pain and suffering on account of ego, attachment, jealousy, pride and so on. During the process of tattwa shuddhi, you imagine the complete transformation of his form taking place within your body, and through this transformation you are actually transforming yourself. This transformation of Papa Purusha should be understood as the inner transformation of the conflict between the negative and positive forces of energy which are striving to unite to awaken the rhythm and balance of the third neutral force.

Transformation of Papa Purusha should be clearly understood in this light. The idea of conflict and disharmony, which gives rise to errors in our personality and nature, is as much physiological as psychological. The two forces of ida and pingala, sun and moon, vital and mental force that are inherent in each being are constantly acting upon each other. Any imbalance between these two forces, ultimately transfers itself to the mental and psychological realm, and vice versa. Therefore, transformation of Papa Purusha is not just an act of cleansing ourselves of sins and vices. That is a purely moral and ethical interpretation and is liable to conjecture. After all, if the act of confessing sins could wash them away, life would be very simple.

Papa Purusha does not mean sinful man, as would be understood from an ethical and religious point of view, but symbolizes all that is conflicting, disharmonious and unbalanced. Tantra emphasizes the necessity of experiencing conflict in order to attain harmony. The dualistic and opposing forces of the universe stand as a basic tenet of tantra and we have to understand them as a necessary phenomenon of the universe.

Tantra talks about duality at all levels of creation. At the highest level there is shiva and shakti. They are two sides of the same coin, and this aspect can be observed in every realm of existence and experience: day and night, sun and moon, heat and cold, love and hate. Without day there can be no knowledge of night. We are only able to distinguish the occurrence of night due to our experience of the day that precedes or follows it.

The principle of ida/pingala is based on the same theory. Ida is represented by the moon, pingala is represented by the sun. Ida stands for mental energy, pingala for pranic or vital energy. Ida is cold, pingala is hot, so on and so forth. Due to their conflicting qualities, they create a sort of 'tension' or 'pull' between each other and this is necessary for the evolution of life.

If there were no tension or conflict, we would cease to evolve. We would remain complacent and inert at the level of tamas. However, due to this conflict a strain is created, and due to the strain we are forever trying to find a balance. In our search for the balance we turn to the spiritual experience, and thus our evolution is pushed higher and higher.

Therefore, the grotesque little man which we create in our bodies is a symbolic creation of the imbalance of energy within the entire system that we call the mind and body. He is not the Devil or Satan. Of course, he is symbolized as such to influence that which is deep-rooted in each and every person. The idea of sin is a part of the collective unconscious which has emerged through the ancestral past, and evokes a strong response.

The image of Papa Purusha is skilfully placed at the point of the practice when you are at the stage of being a witnesser, detached from a part of your mind, watching every act and

99

every thought, and assessing your reactions objectively. It is only when you view yourself objectively that you see many facets to your personality which your ego had previously concealed from you, causing you to turn away from that repugnant part of your personality, which you were ashamed to confess you had.

However, tantra says, "No!" You must be able to see yourself as you really are, not as you would like to think you are. You should have the strength and the willpower to face up to your weaknesses as well as your strengths. It is only when you look at yourself that you can begin to do something about it; not a superficial look, not just a glance, but a deep penetrating glare into yourself. Then you yourself will know what to do, and that knowledge is inner knowledge which cannot be attained unless you look within.

Consequently, practices were developed in which the aspirant was taught to look into himself. Some of these practices related to the subconscious and unconscious mind, by placing mandalas before it, because a mandala has the power to attract what exists in those realms of the mind.

Tattwa shuddhi is one such practice in which the mandalas created are related to both parts of your personality, one transcendental and the other severely gross, and you, the aspirant, are asked to decide with which one you wish to unite and identify. However, before asking you to look at yourself, you are given a set of practices that evolve the lowest tattwa of the body into the highest tattwa of the mind. Only when you are established in that state of higher mind are you asked to decide, because that decision will be the accurate decision. Whether to identify with Papa Purusha or Devi; that is the decision you are asked to make. You are not asked to judge yourself through a gross mind, but through a higher mind. This is important. Tattwa shuddhi asks you to wait until the clarity of inner vision reveals itself because that force is much more powerful and accurate.

So, you make a choice according to the level of mind you have attained through the practice. If your practice takes you very deep into yourself, you identify with Devi, but if it is unable to take you so high, then you identify with the grosser level, i.e. Papa Purusha. It all depends on how deep you are capable of going. The practice of tattwa shuddhi shows the way by making you aware that prithvi, apas, agni, vayu and akasha tattwas are only the effects and not the cause. Unless you go back to the cause you cannot discover the root of your being. Therein lies the answer.

Papa Purusha

14

Bhasma: the Bath of Fire

The application of bhasma or ashes forms an integral part of tattwa shuddhi sadhana, as it is symbolic of purification on the physical, as well as subtle and causal realms. Mahayogi Shiva, who is considered to be the father of tantra, is depicted naked and his whole body is besmeared with bhasma. Thus it is considered to be an auspicious act for discovering your shiva nature.

Bhasma literally means 'disintegration'. Any matter which is disintegrated or broken up through the process of fire or water, etc., is considered to be reduced to its 'bhasmic' form. When this process is completed, the residual substance is known as bhasma, which can be considered to be infinitely more refined and pure than the original matter. Thus, through a process of disintegration, the essence behind matter devoid of all its impurities is discovered.

This process of disintegration is significant for it represents the equivalent experience of disintegration of objective awareness as it occurs in tattwa shuddhi. Just as we reduce matter to its bhasmic form externally, in the same way we utilize the 'fire' of this tantric practice to discover the essence which is responsible for this body/mind with all its subtle manifestations. The result of this disintegration is in the form of an inner experience.

Matter has to be disintegrated in several stages to discover its essential nature and each stage reveals a residue which is subtler and finer. Similarly, there are many stages through which we have to travel in order to fully disintegrate the objective self, to experience the otherwise obscured essence. These stages, which are known as pratyahara, dharana and dhyana, induce an experience that gradually grows subtler and subtler, culminating in the fragrance of samadhi, the ultimate essence.

It is the grossness of matter that obscures the subtle essence inherent in it. As such, disintegration is a vital factor in all processes that deal with purification, whether external or internal. Purification implies the elimination of all the dross and impurities, not the addition of any external element. Therefore, the application of bhasma is symbolic because it represents the culmination of the process through which your inner awareness travels on its journey from matter to pure consciousness. At the same line, it also symbolizes the transience of life; as it is said in the Bible, "From dust to dust, ashes to ashes . . ."

Bhasma is widely used in India as a medicinal treat-ment in the system of Ayurveda, one of the oldest and most profound medical systems for the rejuvenation of life. Bhasma can be made from gold, silver, copper or any other metal with curative properties. However, in the practice of tattwa shuddhi, bhasma is prepared from cow dung. The Sanskrit word for cow dung is *gobar* or *go-maya* which literally means 'gift from the cow'. During your travels in India, you may often have noticed the village women making round cakes out of gobar and leaving them to dry outside. It is these cakes that go into the making of bhasma.

The use of gobar is manifold in India. Its inherent properties are a boon for overcoming many ailments. Admittedly, the faeces of most animals, and even human beings for that matter, are a source of disease and bacterial infection. However, on scientific analysis it has been found that the faeces of a cow are not only free from virus and infection, but also contain useful hormones that have germicidal properties. In many South American countries a mixture of cow dung has been used to fight foot-and-mouth disease, which is caused by a certain virus, and this mixture has proved effective in fighting the epidemic.

If this cow dung system does not convince you of its hygienic and mystical properties, then you may completely do away with the practice. However, it is necessary to mention that many appliances, which you use with pride and utmost faith in your daily life, are unhygienic and culturally dangerous, but you never question them on scientific grounds. Even medicines are no exception, often being made from many unhygienic elements. Gobar cannot be compared with these so-called medical and beauty items.

Moreover, the application of bhasma is not just limited to the physical dimensions of man's existence, rather its effects are more tangible on the subtle and causal realms of his consciousness. In yogic parlance, the word *go* is symbolic of the senses. Thus, *Gopal*, a name for Lord Krishna, means 'protector of the senses'. Another name of Krishna, *Govinda*, literally means 'Lord of the senses'. Similarly, *gochar*, which is symbolically used as the field where cows graze, literally means 'the field of the senses', where the objective experiences are taking place.

From this diverse symbology arose the word 'go' or 'gomata' for cow. *Gomata* means 'creator of the senses' which, as we have seen earlier, is none other than prakriti. Thus the cow is revered in India.

Therefore, the reason why gobar and no other substance is used in the practice of tattwa shuddhi is significant. Through the disintegration of gobar by agni or fire, we reduce it to its bhasmic form, which is symbolic of the annihilation or disintegration of the senses. This is precisely what we are trying to do in tattwa shuddhi. Through pratyahara we break up the experiences of the objective world or senses, through dharana we concentrate the residual experience, giving it a subtler form, and through dhyana we further explode the subtle experiences

104

into their original cosmic essence or shiva consciousness. Thus the process of transformation of gobar to bhasma, and application of the residual essence, is parallel to the process which we are trying to create through tattwa shuddhi, thus emphasizing the importance of both exoteric and esoteric practices.

During the practice, the bhasma is applied to the forehead, with mantras, in a specified manner. There are different mantras for householders and sannyasins. The application of ash is the final stage of the practice and the personal experience of all those who have used it, is that it leaves the aspirant with a deep feeling of being cleansed.

On the spiritual level as well, the application of bhasma is used to attract the higher forces of nature. In India, we may see many sadhus and yogis with their bodies besmeared with bhasma, mainly for this purpose. In the *Shiva Purana*, as well as the *Srimad Devi Bhagavatam*, it is stated that those who seek moksha or liberation should use bhasma and wear the rudraksha mala.

However, the ultimate effect of applying bhasma cannot be fully conveyed through words; this practice has to be experienced personally. Words are limiting and have evolved through a process of logic, whereas experience sometimes defies even logic. The important factor is that bhasma has been tried and tested by so many yogis and rishis and its benefits have been verified by all. That is why this practice still continues until today. Yoga has proved to be a thoroughly scientific system of the body and mind, and it is hardly likely that they would accept or advocate the practice of applying bhasma if it did not induce the required effects in the person who uses it.

Preparation of bhasma

As the application of bhasma is considered a vital part of tattwa shuddhi, the method of preparation is detailed below. Bhasma should be prepared a few days prior to the practice and stored in a closed jar ready for use.

Stage 1

1. Take a medium quantity of cow dung and prepare several flat, round cakes.
2. Dry them thoroughly outside in the sun.
3. After they are completely dry, burn them in a large vessel, by igniting a few of the cakes. The fire will automatically spread to the other cakes. Do not light them all at once, as the flame should be slow and moderate. This should be done outdoors, as a lot of fumes will emanate.
4. When they are completely burnt, allow them to cool.
5. Then collect the ash and strain it through a thin muslin cloth. The residue will be a fine grey-black powder or ash.
6. This is the end of stage 1 and the bhasma is ready to use. However, for those who wish to have a more purified and aromatic residue, one more stage can be included.

Stage 2

1. Take the residue from stage 1 and add some cow's milk and ghee (clarified butter made from cow's milk).
2. Make a smooth paste, taking care that it should not become too watery, and then roll the paste into several medium-sized balls.
3. Leave these to dry for a few days, and when they are completely dry, burn them as in stage 1.
4. Strain the residue through a thin muslin cloth. The residue this time will be finer and lighter in colour.
5. Stage 2 can be repeated eleven times, with an addition of milk and ghee each time. With each successive burning the residue will become finer and more white, and the aroma will be as good as any expensive French perfume.
6. After the final stage, store the bhasma in a closed jar, so that the aroma does not escape.

The significance of burning the gobar eleven times is due to the fact that the numerical equivalent of the shiva consciousness is eleven and, therefore, after burning the gobar eleven times, the residue is as subtle and fragrant as the experience of pure consciousness.

15

Practising Tattwa Shuddhi Sadhana

The ideal way to begin tattwa shuddhi sadhana, as stated in the *Srimad Devi Bhagavatam*, is to make a *sankalpa* or resolve under the auspices of a guru to do this practice for a specified number of days. It is said that the sankalpa can be made for twelve, six or three years, or one year, six months, twelve, six, three, or at least one day. The duration you choose to do it for should be on the basis of your ability, willpower and mental resolve to fulfil the sankalpa. Once it is made, a sankalpa should never be broken, so the decision should be given a great deal of thought prior to starting.

The practice can be started any time of the year. However, for more effective results, it is advisable to begin during *Shravan* (July–August) or *Ashwin* (October). Ashwin is a special month for Devi worship and the practice is especially auspicious during this period.

The first important factor that an aspirant has to pay heed to is his diet. During any prolonged meditation, diet is very important for several reasons. Firstly, the catabolic, metabolic and anabolic rates of the body undergo a change and therefore the food has to be adjusted accordingly. Heavy food becomes difficult to digest and interferes with the sensitivity and receptivity of higher energy vibrations. Heavy meals tend to make both the body and mind sluggish. Therefore, the diet has to be regulated according to the intensity of the practice.

107

If the practice is done as an intense sadhana for a few days, then the diet should consist of only fruits and milk or yoghurt taken once a day. No condiments such as salt or spice, or beverages should be included in the diet, as they have a stimulating effect on the digestive system, which could create hyperacidity and increase the metabolic and heart rates. In order to avoid the pangs of hunger and a general feeling of weakness and lethargy, one should become accustomed to light meals of fruit, milk and boiled vegetables a few days prior to the practice. In this way, the stomach will be prepared and easily adjust itself to a regulated diet during the period of practice.

In the case of tattwa shuddhi sadhana as a daily discipline after your hatha yoga, kriya yoga or kundalini yoga practices, or even as a daily pooja or ritual, it is not possible to maintain such strict and stringent rules about diet, in view of the pressures of work and family situations. In such instances one may maintain the sadhana under the conditions most suitable.

The aspirant who wishes to do this practice need not become alarmed at the idea of such a frugal diet. In fact, we have to understand that it is prana which feeds the whole body with energy and nourishment. It is on prana that we live, breathe and move. A person who is low in prana cannot maintain good health, even if he has the most nutritious diet recommended by the best doctors. Without prana he will not even be able to digest or assimilate food. Therefore, a few days on fruit and milk cannot affect him adversely, rather it will do him good.

Through tattwa shuddhi one is increasing the level of prana and channelling it throughout the body. In fact, if done correctly, the aspirant may even gain weight in spite of fasting. In the final analysis, it is not how much you eat, but how much your body can assimilate that is important. When the pranic systems in the body are revitalized, the processes of assimilation and digestion are spontaneously corrected and recharged.

In the *Srimad Devi Bhagavatam* it is emphasized that the head should be shaved prior to the practice, the reason for this being that during intense practices of meditation, the heat in the body increases and needs a proper channel for release. If the hair is long, it obstructs the escape of heat and gives rise to skin eruptions or it will overheat some other part of the body system. Shaving the head may not be possible for everyone, but those who do not face any restrictions should try to do so.

It is also a good practice to wear an unstitched cloth during the time of sadhana, such as that worn by sannyasins. This cloth can be pure white, geru or ochre. These colours have been known to have a deep influence on the unconscious levels of the mind, and you will discover for yourself that they create a positive atmosphere for spiritual experience. An unstitched cloth is symbolic of vairagya or dispassion, which has been declared by saints and sages as a necessary state of mind for higher spiritual experience. Even the greatest exponent of raja yoga, Sage Patanjali, has clearly enumerated in his *Yoga Sutras* that vairagya is one of the basic tenets through which the mind can attain one-pointedness.

Therefore, it is necessary to develop the sublime notion of vairagya to all external, as well as internal attitudes, if not at all times, at least during the hours of sadhana. Those of you who wish to inculcate this feeling during the time of sadhana should experiment by wearing the prescribed cloth.

Although many of the disciplines which are enumerated here may seem absurd, and the reader may regard them as unnecessary external rituals, it is worthwhile to try them out for yourself before dismissing them so lightly. External rites and rituals have a deeper influence on us than we can imagine or accept. They influence the realms of the mind that we are trying to reach through sadhana and, as those realms are beyond logic, it is hard to define the exact effect they will produce. So, for the time being, let us say that these disciplines influence the spiritual samskaras in us to flower and unfold from within.

Moreover, as a sadhaka in search of inner experience, it is imperative that you should try to discard all the mental conditioning that has been inflicted on you by society. Society has brainwashed you to live, eat, sleep, dress and think in a particular manner, but it has never occurred to you that these conditionings act against your spiritual growth as they are the basis of all raga and dwesha, i.e. attachments, likes and dislikes.

Traditional stipulations

Traditionally, tattwa shuddhi should be practised three times a day; during the hours of *brahmamuhurta* (4–6 a.m.), at midday, and at *sandhya* or dusk. Prior to each practice, you should bathe and clean yourself thoroughly. You should select a quiet place for the practice, preferably a room which is not subject to intrusion. The room should be kept simple and bare, and before each session you should clean it thoroughly. The items required for the practice are a comfortable mat, oil lamp, incense or sandal, flowers, an offering of food (sweetmeats – preferably something you have prepared) and a bowl of water for the application of bhasma. The bhasma should be prepared beforehand and kept in a jar.

On the appointed day, you should wake up early, bathe and sit down for the practice, facing towards the north or east. Before beginning the practice, you should light the oil lamp and incense and mentally repeat your sankalpa. After this, you can begin to practise and continue it in this manner three times a day for the appointed number of days. On the last day, you should practise *mouna* (silence) and after the last session at dusk sit down for a special meditation on the formless reality.

Tattwa shuddhi as a regular meditational practice

Tattwa shuddhi can be practised in two ways, either as an intensive sadhana for a fixed number of days, at least once a year, or as a daily discipline along with hatha yoga, kriya yoga or any form of tantric meditation. For those who are still searching for a way to meditate, this could be an ideal way to begin because tattwa shuddhi is a bridge between the exoteric and esoteric practices of tantra and yoga.

The stipulations of fasting, diet and so on need not be imposed when it is not practised as an intense sadhana. Then it should be performed only once a day. However, one can use the external rituals of lighting an oil lamp and incense to create a suitable atmosphere at the time of practice.

One should also meditate at the same time and place every day. Regular timing is an essential discipline, as it creates a particular biorhythm and an involuntary reflex in the brain and body. Certain timings are more conducive for spiritual practices, and these are mainly between 4 and 6 a.m. and before going to sleep in the evening. This practice can also be undertaken at midnight by those who are adventurous.

Tattwa shuddhi is particularly effective before yantra or mandala meditation. In fact, in tantra it is emphasized as a preliminary rite before yantra and mandala pooja. Through tattwa shuddhi sadhana the practitioner transcends the mundane awareness and through the higher forces awakened in him, he invokes power into the yantra or mandala, which then begins to reveal its inherent force.

The practice of tattwa shuddhi should eventually become a part of your daily discipline, as a cleansing process. Just as you bathe and brush your teeth every day as a necessary routine for physical hygiene, tattwa shuddhi sadhana should become a routine procedure for mental, psychic and spiritual hygiene. Your physical body collects dirt and filth if it is not cleaned every day and, in the same way, the subtler levels of your being accumulate dross in the form of samskaras. If they are not taken care of, they will affect the entire structure of your life. The subtle elements of the body and mind have to be 'overhauled' just as you overhaul your car. Only after this process of purification is perfected can *sthiti* or illumination become possible.

111

Guidelines for intensive sadhana

The mental attitude during any prolonged sadhana is of paramount importance. During intensive sadhana, the perception becomes very sensitive and one develops extreme clarity of mind and tremendous psychic power. This force has to be used correctly and creatively. If you are not careful about this, the same power can become a negative force, destroying the strengths and experiences you have built up through your sadhana. During the practice, strong emotions may arise, disturbing thoughts can torment you, minor incidents can upset or irritate you, but you should have the strength and zeal to remain undisturbed by them.

Tell yourself that at least during the period of your sankalpa, you will maintain the balance by not allowing events to affect you. Try to remain a witness or sakshi, observing each and every moment of your day. Mentally detach yourself and know what is taking place in your mind, instead of being involved in the gamut of emotions, feelings and frustrations which attack your mental stability through a direct onslaught. It is only when you achieve the act of witnessing that the process of purging the samskaras begins, and the energy force of the emotions is channelled creatively to arouse inner experience.

Mouna is also a helpful practice to inculcate during intensive sadhana. Just as fasting cleanses the physical body, so mouna purifies the mind. Unnecessary chatter and gossip externalizes the mind and the inner experience can be lost, but through mouna you intensify inner awareness. You travel within and witness the subtle workings within the body, mind and psyche. Therefore, the practitioner is advised to select at least one day for the observance of mouna.

The observance of mouna, fasting and intense sadhana does not imply that you should become inactive. On the contrary, you should make it a point to do some work, retiring to rest only if it is absolutely necessary. In fact, while performing tattwa shuddhi as an intensive sadhana, you should not stay idle either physically or mentally, but go

112

about your household chores as usual, trying to do a little more than normal. This helps to keep the mind engaged, thus avoiding all unnecessary thoughts which disturb the mental equilibrium. It also does not mean that you should stop your previous sadhana. If you are practising hatha yoga, kriya yoga or any other sadhana, you should continue these practices. You will derive greater results by incorporating both sadhanas.

The hours of sleeping also have to be regulated. A minimum of five hours and a maximum of seven hours is advisable during the intense practice of tattwa shuddhi. Sleep is one of the first obstacles in yoga because as the mind becomes introvert, the first by-product is relaxation and this induces a momentary dullness and sleep ensues. In fact, sometimes it becomes difficult to stay awake. Halfway through the practice you find yourself dropping off to sleep. This is one of the reasons why a bath (preferably cold) before the practice is necessary. However, if you find that you still cannot keep awake, stop your practice, splash your face with cold water and continue the practice, or even start again if the concentration is disturbed.

Intellect, an obstacle in sadhana

It has been stated time and again in all the textbooks on tantra and yoga that an aspirant should try to eliminate all intellectual barriers in respect to his spiritual sadhana. As long as you approach your sadhana through an intellectual process of logic and reasoning, your experiences will remain static. The level of mind that you are trying to reach is beyond the entanglements of intellectual bantering. Questions such as, "Why am I doing this sadhana?" "What do these visions mean?" "Am I making any progress?" "Where are all these experiences coming from?" "Where will all this lead me?" are bound to arise in every person. However, these and other intellectual acrobatics have to be avoided.

Use your intellect for your worldly day to day life by all means because it is necessary and serves a purpose. However, in sadhana, this same faculty becomes a hindrance and is an obstacle. That is why Sri Aurobindo has said, "Intellect was the helper, intellect is the barrier; transcend intellect." This should be the motto of all sadhakas. Intellect is all right up to a point; it is through discrimination of your intellect that you began the practices of yoga. However, in order to go higher you will now have to step over it. This may not be possible all the time, but should be maintained at all cost during the period of intensive sadhana.

Faith, love and devotion are the mediums through which the higher experiences begin to manifest, because these qualities absorb and nullify the cold and calculated reasoning of the intellect. Therefore, let us approach this sadhana, not through the severity of the intellect but through the trans- forming emotions of bhakti. In the *Srimad Devi Bhagavatam*, Devi says that jnana and bhakti are the two pathways that lead to her. Try not to hinder your progress by the process of analysis. Drop these tendencies, which exist in every ordi- nary person, and try to enter the realm of pure experience by elevating the awareness beyond the barriers of intellect through bhakti or devotion.

Practice of tattwa shuddhi

Tattwa shuddhi is enumerated in several tantric texts as it is an integral part of tantric sadhana. However, the methods delineated are often very abstract and at times impossible for the average practitioner to accomplish. In some texts it is stated that one should concentrate on prithvi tattwa for five *ghatikas* (two hours) while performing *antar kumbhaka* or inner retention; on the water tattwa for ten *nadikas* (four hours) while performing inner retention of breath, and in this way, right up to the last tattwa, which is meditated on for several hours.

It is easy to see that anyone less than a yogi would fail to accomplish even a fraction of the practice as stipulated in such texts. For this reason, the practice detailed here has been especially adapted for the benefit of the average person

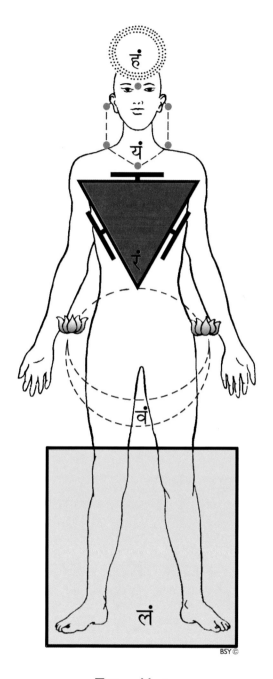

Tattwa Yantras

who has neither the time nor the stamina for such long hours of sadhana. The source of the sadhana described here is the *Srimad Devi Bhagavatam*, but the basic guidelines and restructuring have been done by Swami Satyananda Saraswati.

Technique
Stage 1: Preparation

Prior to beginning the practice of tattwa shuddhi, it is advisable to develop pratyahara through the practice of trataka or pranayama. This helps in steadying the mind and going deep within.

After ten to fifteen minutes of trataka or pranayama, one should keep the eyes closed.

Practise kaya sthairyam in a comfortable and steady sitting position, preferably siddhasana, siddha yoni asana or padmasana.

Visualize the form of your guru, whoever he or she may be. Mentally pay obeisance to him/her as it is through his/her will that you are doing the practice.

Now bring your awareness to mooladhara chakra and imagine the kundalini shakti rising up through sushumna nadi to sahasrara chakra at the crown of the head.

Then meditate on the mantra *Hamso*, synchronizing it with the outgoing and ingoing breath. *Ham* with exhalation down sushumna, from sahasrara to mooladhara; *So* with inhalation up sushumna, from mooladhara to sahasrara. Feel the downward and upward movement with the mantra *Hamso* as the movement of your inner consciousness, your inner spirit. With each breath feel yourself becoming united with Brahman (supreme consciousness).

Stage 2: Creation of the tattwa yantras

Now take your awareness to that part of your physical body between the toes and the knees. Visualize there the shape of a large, luminous yellow square, which is the yantra of prithvi tattwa, the earth element. See its golden colour. Feel its solidity and weight. As you visualize the square, mentally repeat the bija mantra *Lam*.

Then move your awareness to the area between the knees and the navel. Visualize there a white crescent moon with an open white lotus at either end. It is surrounded by a circle of water. This is the yantra of apas tattwa, the water element. While gazing at the white crescent moon, mentally repeat the bija mantra *Vam*.

Now move your awareness to the region between the navel and the heart. Imagine there a bright red inverted triangle made of fire, with a bhupura on each outer side. This is the yantra of agni tattwa, the fire element. As you visualize it, mentally repeat the bija mantra *Ram*.

Next take your awareness to the region between the heart and the eyebrow centre. Imagine there six grey-blue gaseous dots forming a hexagonal shape. This is the yantra of vayu tattwa, the air element. It has a smoky hue. As you visualize the blue-grey hexagon, mentally repeat the bija mantra *Yam*.

Then move your awareness to the region between the eyebrow centre and the crown of the head. Imagine there the circular yantra of akasha tattwa, the ether element. Within this circular form is a total void, shoonya. It is black and may be filled with multi-coloured dots. As you gaze into the void, mentally repeat the bija mantra *Ham*.

Stage 3: Dissolution of the tattwas

After creating these tattwas, take your awareness back down to the prithvi yantra. See its form becoming liquid and dissolving into apas, apas into agni, agni into vayu, and vayu into akasha.

Now imagine akasha dissolving into ahamkara, the ego, its cause. Then feel ahamkara dissolving into mahat tattwa, the great principle, and mahat tattwa dissolving into prakriti, and prakriti into the supreme self, purusha. Then consider yourself as being the highest knowledge, pure and absolute.

Stage 4: Transformation of the lower nature

Now take your awareness down to the left side of the abdomen and visualize there a little man, the size of your thumb. He is known as Papa Purusha. His skin is black as coal; he has fiery eyes and a large belly. In one hand he holds an axe and in the other a shield. His whole form is grotesque.

Now transform this little man through your breath and the use of mantra.

Close your right nostril with your right thumb and inhale through the left nostril while repeating the bija mantra *Yam* four times. See this little man becoming clean and white. His whole face and figure is being transformed.

Closing both nostrils, perform breath retention and repeat the bija mantra *Ram* four times. See this little man being burnt to ashes.

Then exhale the ashes through the right nostril, while repeating the bija mantra *Vam* four times. See the ashes rolling into a ball and mixing with the nectar from the moon in the water yantra.

Now, repeating the bija mantra *Lam*, see this little ball in the left side of your abdomen being transformed into a golden egg.

Repeat the bija mantra *Ham* and visualize the golden egg growing and glowing until it fills your entire body, and you become the golden egg itself. Feel as if you are reborn.

Stage 5: Reconstruction of the tattwas

Then begin to recreate the elements in the reverse order. From the golden egg, again become the supreme self, then prakriti, then mahat tattwa, then ahamkara.

From ahamkara, see akasha yantra emerge; from akasha, vayu; from vayu, agni; from agni, apas; from apas, prithvi. Locate the tattwa yantras in their respective positions represented by their bija mantras, as described earlier.

Stage 6: Return of kundalini to mooladhara

When all the elements are reconstructed, repeat the mantra *Soham* in sushumna once more, moving your awareness with the breath between mooladhara and sahasrara. With each breath feel you are again separating the jivatma, or individual soul, from paramatma, or the cosmic soul, and locate the jivatma in the heart region where it resides.

Now visualize the kundalini shakti, which you had raised to sahasrara, returning back to mooladhara via sushumna, piercing each chakra as it descends.

Stage 7: The form of Shakti

Then take your awareness to chidakasha.

See before you a vast, deep red ocean with a large red lotus on it. Seated on that lotus is the form of Prana Shakti (the vital life force). Her body is the colour of the rising sun and is decorated with beautiful ornaments.

She has three eyes, and six arms. In her first hand she holds a trident; in the second, a bow made from sugarcane; in the third, a noose; in the fourth, a goad; in the fifth, five arrows; and in the sixth, a skull dripping with blood.

Continue to gaze at her glorious form and say to yourself, "May she grant us happiness."

Stage 8: Application of bhasma

Become aware of yourself seated on the floor. Develop complete body awareness. Breathe in slowly and deeply and open your eyes.

Thus, having meditated, one should apply bhasma.

Take some bhasma on your middle and ring fingers and slowly wipe two lines on your forehead, moving the hand from left to right and repeating the mantra *Om Hraum Namah Shivaya*. (Sannyasins should repeat the mantra *Om Hamsah*.)

Then, taking some more ashes on the thumb, wipe a line from right to left above the other two, repeating the same mantra. (The bhasma should be slightly wet when applying before midday and dry after midday.)

Thus feel yourself to be purified.

16

Effects of Tattwa Shuddhi Sadhana

Tantra considers that shakti, the active energy principle in each and every speck of creation, grants favours easily. As tattwa shuddhi is a tantric upasana done to shakti, the results have been known to be quicker and more powerful than other sadhanas. These results accrue as both material gain and psychic powers or siddhis. Though the results come without much difficulty, if they are not properly utilized, they can cause a serious imbalance in the aspirant and ultimately lead to destruction of spiritual growth. This is why the shastras emphasize that the practice should only be done after initiation by the guru.

It is also necessary to mention here that the lasting effects of any practice depend entirely on the regularity with which it is done. In the *Yoga Sutras* of Sage Patanjali it is stated that *abhyasa* or constant uninterrupted practice is one of the necessary foundations on which the unfoldment of spiritual experience depends. Therefore, it is not so important how much you practise, but how regularly you practise it.

What we are trying to do through the practices of tantra is to train the mind, intellect and consciousness, to behave in a particular manner and under the control of our will. However, in order to do this it is important to maintain discipline in the form of regularity. The consciousness which is travelling through varying stages in its journey towards illumination requires a certain momentum in order to propel

119

it forward, otherwise all the efforts that you have put into your sadhana are nullified, as the consciousness can at any time regress into gross awareness if the sadhana is disrupted.

In tantra it is not accumulation of knowledge that we are trying to attain, but experience. Knowledge once gained is stored somewhere in the depths of your memory and cannot be lost. If you resume your education, which stopped at a certain point, you will start from where you left off. However, inner experience follows a different set of rules altogether. You cannot just start at the point where your sadhana was disrupted, you have to start from the beginning.

Therefore, to evolve through any sadhana we have to make constant and unceasing efforts to keep alive what we have already gained. The practice of tattwa shuddhi has the potential to take the aspirant very deep into himself, but for that, regularity is of paramount importance.

Physical effects

The practice of tattwa shuddhi brings about subtle changes in the consciousness, which become evident to the practitioner on the physical, mental, emotional, psychic and spiritual levels. On the physical level, the combination of fasting and the dynamic practices of tattwa shuddhi work together to reorganize and transform the entire physical body. We have seen how the physical elements or tattwas reverberate throughout the body to compose our present structure of flesh, blood and bones. Therefore, when we re-energize and purify the tattwas, the effects are spontaneously transferred to the grosser organs such as the heart, liver, kidneys, pancreas and all the organs which have arisen out of the tattwas.

The effects on the body can be felt through a transformation of the metabolic, catabolic and anabolic rates which are so vital for the sound functioning of the physical body. This leads to the regeneration and energizing of the tissues and cells which create a healthy body and mind. In turn, this results in an experience of lightness and suppleness, and the skin regains its lustre.

The application of bhasma has a cooling effect on the entire body and nervous system. It eliminates excessive heat that may have been created by intensive meditation practice, or even the heat produced by faulty diet and the malfunctioning of the inner organs. Bhasma also helps all bodily wounds to disappear thus making the skin glow radiantly. It is for this reason that the *Srimad Devi Bhagavatam* states that, "Through this sankalpa one can avoid the occurrence of leprosy, fistulae and other phlegmatic diseases." Just as through the hatha yoga practice of shankhaprakshalana we thoroughly cleanse the internal organs, through tattwa shuddhi we create an effect of shankaprakshalana on the entire network of the energy system in the body and mind. The chakras and numerous nadis are cleared of blockages which prevent the free flow of energy, and the quantity of energy is increased. As a result all the bodily processes are spontaneously rejuvenated.

Effects on the mind

The mind also plays a very important role in influencing the bodily processes. Thoughts have been known to have the power to generate a disease on the physical level. We have seen how many heart failures are a result of anxiety and stress. In tattwa shuddhi we use the force of the mind and imagination to superimpose the tattwas on the physical body in their pristine purity, and with the force of the mind we follow the whole process of evolution and involution of the subtle energy fields in the body. After all, the mind is also made up of tattwas which are in fact more subtle and powerful compared to those that manifest in the physical body. Therefore, we use the stronger forces of the mind to create a tangible and positive effect on a weaker force, the body.

On the mental and emotional levels, tensions and preconceived notions drop away, due to the heightened level of prana and the resulting harmony of the energy systems. During the practice of meditation, one is often disturbed by the 'goings-on' in the subconscious mind which might come up to the surface. The *Srimad Devi Bhagavatam* states that, "This practice saves one from demons and ghosts." These are all the suppressions and repressions of the past which have to be expelled, but how can we do it without disturbing the concentration? In tattwa shuddhi, it is found that in spite of visions the mind remains calm and tranquil. This inner balance can be felt even after the practice. It is a sense of equilibrium and equipoise which does not become disturbed by negative external influences. Moreover, the samskaras which cause you to react to any situation are expelled with greater speed through tattwa shuddhi sadhana. When the samskara is not there, how can it create a disturbing influence?

Through visualization and concentration on the tattwa yantras, chanting of the mantras and creating mandalas, the samskaras are purged from within through dreams, visions and thoughts which travel to the conscious mind. Psychic visions are a result of most yoga practices, but in tattwa shuddhi they become more acute. These psychic visions can be experienced as subtle sounds, smell, touch, tastes or forms, and due to the heightened inner awareness one becomes sensitive to their existence.

The psychic dimension of man's experience is as real as the physical dimension. The only difference is that due to the gross level of awareness they remain unnoticed. This act of purging on the psychic level leaves one relatively free from mental and emotional turmoil. It is only when one becomes free from physical and mental tension that the subtler spiritual experiences begin to manifest.

Siddhis and spiritual benefit

The yoga shastras clearly state that siddhis can be attained by concentration on the tattwas. In the *Gherand Samhita* it is said that, absorbing the mind and prana in prithvi tattwa induces steadiness of body and mind; in apas tattwa it destroys pain and suffering; in agni tattwa it eradicates the fear of death; in vayu it enables flying; and in akasha tattwa it paves the way to liberation. Apart from this, awakening of the tattwas develops the higher faculties of clairvoyance, clairaudience, telepathy and intuition.

Prithvi tattwa helps cure disease and makes the body light and subtle. In fact, levitation can even take place by mastering this element. Apas tattwa equalizes the flow of prana vayu and when activated it enables astral travelling. Agni tattwa induces the ability to transform base metals into gold and enter somebody else's physical body. Awakening of vayu tattwa brings knowledge of the past, present and future, contact with astral entities, and the ability of psychic healing. Akasha tattwa enables psychic projection and reveals metaphysical truths. However, the aim for which we are trying to activate the tattwas is higher spiritual experience and not the acquisition of these powers.

In terms of spiritual experience, this practice leads to heightened awareness of the subtle forces pervading the entire cosmos. The same mental frequencies which were responsible for gross, objective experience are raised to the tune of the finer vibrations in the whole cosmos, so that one begins to experience unity both within and without. This is due to the fact that one begins to respond to these forces with greater clarity and intuition, and thus the knowledge which can be gained from them is spontaneously transferred to the conscious mind. These effects occur as a natural consequence of the practice and one does not have to labour very hard to understand what the inner faculties are trying to tell us. One becomes naturally intuitive and a feeling of bliss is felt on all levels.

The tantric texts also state that knowledge of the tattwas generates the highest dispassion. The quality of vairagya or dispassion develops as a consequence of the realization that all matter is transient and that the human form is just an aggregate of atoms, molecules and particles of energy. This knowledge inculcates a sense of detachment, for it is impossible to feel attachment and passion towards objects and persons when they are realized as conglomerations of energy. This detachment is the soil for the seed of vairagya.

All of the above observations are based on the personal experiences and experiments conducted by sincere sadhakas who have undergone this sadhana for extended periods. As the practice of tattwa shuddhi has remained more or less obscured from most yoga practitioners and sadhakas, particularly in the occident, we have not yet been able to validate the above claims through scientific experiments. Nevertheless recent research on meditation, mantra, yantra, mandala and fasting are sufficient to testify to the efficacy of this practice.

17

Guru

In the *Shiva Samhita* (3:11), it states, "Only the knowledge imparted by a guru, through his lips, is powerful and useful, otherwise it becomes fruitless, weak and very painful." In fact, all the ancient texts state that for spiritual sadhana, especially the higher esoteric practices, the guru is indispensable. From all points of view this is a logical claim. We need the guidance of a teacher to gain knowledge of all faculties or sciences. Then why doubt the necessity of a guide for the spiritual sciences?

Guru means 'one who dispels the darkness', i.e. ignorance, and brings illumination. Therefore, the guru is more than just a teacher. A teacher can only give you academic knowledge to satisfy and stimulate your intellect but the guru gives you intuitive knowledge through intimate experience. He is one who has realized his true Self by the dint of his own sadhana and rigorous disciplines. He has travelled the same path which we are stumbling along and knows the pitfalls and dangers that may befall the disciple.

The path is hazardous, narrow as a razor's edge and few who have traversed it know the way. We are not even sure of the destination, so how can we assume to know the way? However, the guru has been there and his return to show us the way is part of his grace which, as sadhakas, we should humbly acknowledge. The divine powers have unfolded in him and revealed the unknown mysteries of spirit. Not only has he discovered the hidden reality for himself, but he can also transmit the experience to others to encourage them on the same path. In fact, such a guru lives for just this purpose: to awaken the yearning for spiritual knowledge in others.

In India, which has upheld the tradition of gurus from time immemorial, a guru is regarded as divinity incarnate. Indians believe that a guru, through his spiritual accomplishment, is the closest thing to God that is amongst us. If God exists, that is all right, but has anyone seen him? The guru is the only manifestation of the divine that we have witnessed and, therefore, he is humbly acknowledged as a guide and preceptor. The greatest intellectuals, thinkers and philosophers have bowed down before a guru who has had the experience of truth, for what is academic knowledge before experience?

As adults in a so-called civilized society, we revere the supremacy of the intellect, thereby ignoring any other source of knowledge, even if it is more accurate. We are not to blame, for that is how we have been trained from childhood, but in spiritual life one has to transcend the intellect and bypass it through the sublime emotions of faith, love and devotion. In order to progress in spiritual life, one has to unlearn everything because the spiritual experience is beyond intellect and does not follow the logical and rational codes of behaviour. This is why one is often told to be as innocent as a child who is not bound by the logical claims of the intellect.

The basis for all spiritual sadhana is the personal evolution of the sadhaka. Culturally, socially, racially and politically we may all be the same; even from the point of view of religion we may be alike, but in terms of spiritual evolution no two persons are at the same point. Who can know at which rung of the ladder you are poised? Your spiritual sadhana has to begin from the point you are at. It is the guru alone who can judge this, by examining the karma and personal evolution of an aspirant, and giving a sadhana on that basis. This insight is very important as your progress depends upon the suitability and efficacy of the practised sadhana.

Very often people complain that they cannot meditate. However, they have failed to understand that without fulfilling the preliminary disciplines to evolve the body and mind meditation is not possible. The body is not capable of maintaining steadiness for more than ten minutes and the mind is continually wavering from one thought to the next. Then how can meditation be possible? The fault is not in the practice of meditation but that you are trying to 'fit a square peg in a round whole'.

Sometimes the aspirant may have already evolved through sadhana done in previous lives, but in order for him to pick up the loose threads he requires the hand of a master craftsman. In spiritual life, the power with which you are playing is the same power that has created you, that of consciousness. A delicate matter, no doubt requiring the skill of a professional. The guru has the skill to do this. Spiritual sadhana can never be chosen on the personal whim of the sadhaka. It is guru alone who has the authority, insight and experience to judge which sadhana is best for an aspirant.

We are all amateurs in the lila or game of life, in spite of which we think we can etch the finest creations. Moreover, the path of spiritual sadhana is through the deepest layers of the mind, where all the skeletons of past experiences are residing. An encounter with them can be dangerous for your equilibrium, if it is not done under the watchful guidance of a guru.

It is the guru who initiates you into sadhana and gives you the inspiration to remain on the path in spite of any difficulties that may assail you. Initiation is an important factor before beginning any sadhana. The guru's initiation is power-charged and creates a suitable atmosphere and mental equilibrium to fulfil the obligations of the spiritual practice and thereby receive the merits of sadhana. It is stated in the tantra shastras that without initiation from a guru, sadhana cannot induce the desired results.

Sadhana given by the guru helps to extract the ego and eliminate the karma of the disciple, if it is practised without expectation. Acceptance of the guru's guidance without anticipation of any merit implies subjugation of your ego. Whatever you decide to do yourself involves the ego. However, when the guru instructs you, it is not your desire but his order that motivates you. When there is no desire, there is no expectation, no delusion, and through this subtle process the disciple evolves.

Glossary

Abhyasa – constant, uninterrupted practice.

Adinatha – the 'first Lord', name given to Lord Shiva by the natha sect of yogis. First guru of the natha yogis and primordial guru of all. Cosmic consciousness.

Aditara – female counterpart of Adinatha.

Agni tattwa – fire element.

Ahamkara – ego; awareness of 'I'; centre of individual mental, emotional, psychic and physical functioning.

Ajapa japa – spontaneous repetition of the mantra.

Akasha tattwa – ether element.

Amsa roopini – partial manifestation of shakti and potential of each chakra; see Dakini, Rakini, Lakini, Sakini and Hakini.

Anandamaya kosha – sheath or body of bliss and supramental consciousness.

Anga nyasa – consecration of the limbs of the body through mantra.

Annamaya kosha – sheath or body made of food.

Antah karana – literally means 'inner tool' or 'inner self; the instrument of consciousness. See Ahamkara, Manas, Chitta, Buddhi.

Antar kumbhaka – internal breath retention. An essential step in the perfection of pranayama.

Anu – described by the yogis as an atom, the anu combine together to form particles of matter.

Apana vayu – pranic air current operating in the abdominal region, causing elimination through the excretory and reproductive organs.

Apas tattwa – water element.

Arpana – unification with the higher force within oneself, or realization of the cosmic consciousness.

Asana – traditionally a comfortable meditative sitting pose; a specific position for balancing and channelling prana.

Ashwin – seventh month of the lunar calendar which begins mid-October and ends mid-November.

Atma – soul or inner spirit. The universal atma (paramatma) manifests as the individual atma (jivatma).

Atma shakti – spiritual force or energy.

Atma shuddhi – purification of the causal body.

Atma tattwa – conditioned elements of the microcosmos which relate to the material universe.

Avidya vidya – one of the kanchukas which restricts the capacity to know.

Avyakta – unmanifest.

Bandha – psychomuscular energy lock which redirects the flow of psychic energy in the body.

Bhairava – an epithet of Lord Shiva, signifying the state which is beyond mundane consciousness.

Bhairavi – feminine counterpart of Bhairava, together these refer to those who have gone beyond dualities.

Bhakti – intense inner devotion or love.

Bhasma – purified essence or ash.

Bhava – intense inner attitude.

Bhu loka – terrestrial plane of existence.

Bhupura – the outer protective force of a yantra which acts as the entrance.

Bhuta – element, tattwa. See Panchatattwa.

Bhuta shuddhi – same as tattwa shuddhi; purification of the five elements.

Bhuvar loka – intermediate realm between heaven and earth.

Bija mantra – seed mantra; a basic mantra; a vibration which has its origin in transcendental consciousness.

Bindu – top back portion of the head. A point or drop which is the substratum of the whole cosmos; the seat of the total creation. In tantra it also refers to a drop of semen.

Brahma jnana – experience and knowledge of Brahma, pure consciousness.

Brahmamuhurta – sattwic time of day between 4 and 6 a.m., best suited for yogic sadhana.

Brahman – etymologically it means 'ever-expanding, limitless consciousness'. Absolute reality; monistic concept of Vedanta.

Buddhi – intellect, also creative intelligence; one of the faculties of the antah karana.

Chakra – literally means 'wheel or vortex'. Major psychic centre in the pranic body, responsible for specific physiological and psychic functions; conjugating point of the nadis.

Chandra swara – flow of breath in the left nostril only.

Chhayopasana – concentration on one's own shadow.

Chidakasha – psychic space in front of the closed eyes, just behind the forehead.

Chit – pure consciousness.

Chit shakti – the kinetic power akin to pure consciousness.

Chitta – memory; one of the faculties of the antah karana. Individual consciousness.

Chitta shakti – the kinetic energy of individual consciousness.

Chitta shuddhi – purification of individual consciousness.

Dakini – shakti of dhatu in mooladhara, one of the amsa roopinis.

Dakshina marga – one of the paths designed by tantra, suitable for aspirants of sattwic nature. Etymologically it means the 'right path'.

Darshan – to see; to have inner vision and blessing of the divine power.

Deva – literally means 'illumined one'; higher force or power.

Deva shuddhi – purification of the psychic body or vijnanamaya kosha.

Devi – a divine force, manifestation of Shakti.

131

Dharana – technique of concentration. Stage when mind is one-pointed and concentrated.

Dhatu – mineral of the body; altogether there are seven. See Sapta Dhatu.

Dhyana – meditation; stage of introversion and concentration of mind in which the meditator and object of meditation come in close range of each other.

Durga – poorna shakti; personification of Shakti in her fearsome aspect.

Dwesha – aversion, dislike.

Gandha tanmatra – the subtle principle or essence of smell.

Gauri – name of Shiva's consort; an epithet for shakti used to denote the awakening or rising of energy.

Ghatika – period of 24 minutes.

Guna – quality of maya, three in number; see tamas, rajas, sattwa.

Guru – spiritually enlightened soul, who by the light of his own atma, can dispel darkness, ignorance and illusion from the mind of a disciple.

Hakini – shakti of the dhatu of ajna chakra; one of the amsa roopinis.

Hatha yoga – a system of yoga specifically dealing with the practices of bodily purification, in which the two poles of energy existing in man's physical body are brought into harmony by a systematic series of practices.

Ida nadi – major pranic/psychic channel in the subtle body which conducts mental energy throughout the body and mind. Located in the left side of the body. The 'tha' of hatha yoga, indicates the moon or lunar force.

Indriya – sense organ; see karmendriya and jnanendriya.

Ishta devata – one's personal symbol; form or vision of divinity.

Jagriti – conscious realm; material world of the senses.

Jana loka – plane of rishis and munis.

Japa – conscious and continual repetition of a mantra.

Jiva – same as jivatma.

Jivatma – individual soul.

Jnanendriya – sense organ of knowledge, five in number; ears, eyes, nose, tongue and skin.

Kaala – one of the kanchukas; limiting aspect of shakti which binds the individual consciousness and body in time and space.

Kakini – shakti of dhatu in anahata chakra; one of the amsa roopinis.

Kalaa – one of the kanchukas; limiting aspect of shakti which restricts the creative power of the individual consciousness and body.

Kali – aspect of poorna shakti, which is the destroyer of time, space and object, i.e. ignorance.

Kanchuka – invisible 'cloak' of shakti or maya which limits or restricts consciousness.

Kara nyasa – consecration of part of hand through mantra.

Karana sharira – causal body.

Karma – action; law of cause and effect. In tantra it refers to the sum total of man's destiny.

Karmendriya – organ of action, five in number; hands, feet, vocal cords/tongue, excretory and reproductive organs.

Kaulachara – practitioner of doctrines of kaula marga tantra.

Kaula marga – a path designed by tantra in which the initiation takes place within the kula or family and is passed on from mother to son.

Kaya sthairyam – steadiness of body; pre-meditative practice.

Kirtan – devotional songs composed of mantras.

Kosha – enveloping body, see annamaya, pranamaya, manomaya, vijnanamaya, anandamaya kosha.

Krishna – eighth incarnation of Vishnu, the cosmic sustainer. The principal figure of the Bhagavad Gita.

Kriya yoga – the practical aspect of kundalini yoga. System of twenty practices to awaken the hidden potential creative force and consciousness.

Kula – heritage, lineage.

Kundalini – often referred to as the serpent power. Man's spiritual energy, capacity and consciousness, lying dormant in most people within mooladhara.

Kundalini yoga – philosophy expounding the awakening of the potential energy and inherent consciousness.

Lakini – shakti of dhatu in manipura chakra, one of the amsa roopinis.

Lata sadhana – tantric sadhana in which an adult female is included as a participant.

Lakshmi – aspect of poorna Shakti; goddess of wealth, consort of Vishnu.

Lila – cosmic game of consciousness and energy.

Lingam – naturally oval-shaped stone; represents the subtle bodies. Shiva lingam is especially venerated as it is a symbol of atma.

Loka – realm of existence.

Maha loka – plane of the saints and siddhas.

Mahanirvana Tantra – one of the sixty-four tantras expounding the practices of kaula marga tantra for householders.

Mahaprana – the great shakti; cosmic energy.

Mahat – buddhi, higher consciousness within an individual which operates through ajna chakra.

Maheshwara – the 'Great Lord', an epithet of Shiva.

Maheshwari – the female counterpart or shakti of Maheshwara.

Maithuna – literally means 'union between two polarities'; in common parlance is known as sexual intercourse. In tantra it is used as a spiritual practice.

Manas – part of the antah karana which creates sankalpa/vikalpa, thought/counter-thought.

Manas shakti – same as chitta shakti.

Mandala – a particular diagram within a circumference which invokes the cosmic power.

Manipura chakra – third pranic/psychic centre along the spinal column, associated with the solar plexus.

Manomaya kosha – body or sheath made of mind and thought.

Mantra – particular subtle sound vibration capable of liberating the energy and consciousness of matter.

Marga – path.

Maya – illusory force inherent in shakti, cause of the phenomenal world.

Moksha – liberation from the cycle of birth and death.

Mooladhara chakra – lowest psychic and pranic centre in human evolution.

Moola prakriti – root of the cosmic, creative and kinetic force.

Mouna – vow of silence.

Mudra – physical, mental, psychic attitude of mind and body which channels the cosmic energy.

Nada – subtle sound vibration; inner sound.

Nadi – river, flow, pranic flow of shakti or energy in the subtle body.

Nadika – same as ghatika.

Narayani – shakti or feminine aspect of Narayana (the sustainer of the cosmos).

Nataraja – literally means 'King of the Dance'; an epithet of Shiva.

Naumukhi mudra – physical, mental, psychic gesture of closing the 'nine gates' of the body by closing the orifices of the face with the fingers and contracting the perineal/cervical and urinary muscles.

Nyasa – act of consecrating the body by use of mantra and external worship.

Om – cosmic vibration of the universe; universal mantra. Same as Aum; represents four states of mind; conscious, subconscious, unconscious and supraconscious or cosmic mind.

Padmasana – basic meditative pose in which you sit with the right foot resting on the left thigh and left foot on the right thigh.

Panchamahabhuta – same as panchatattwa; the five elements.

Panchatattwa – the five elements of ether, air, fire, water and earth. See akasha, vayu, agni, apas, prithvi tattwa.

Panchavayu – the five pranic air currents; see prana, apana, samana, udana, vyana vayu.

Panchikara – process of converting subtle elements into gross elements.

Panchopchara – diffusion of one element into another by exoteric rites and offerings; part of rishyadi nyasa.

Para – greatest, supreme, transcendental.

Para sadhana – highest form of sadhana.

Para shakti – the great cosmic kinetic principle.

Paramtattwa – the greatest and first element.

Parinama – change, growth, evolution.

Parvati – kinetic principle or Shakti, consort of Shiva.

Patanjali, Sage – propounder of the yoga philosophy and ashtanga yoga; author of the Yoga Sutras.

Pinda – cage, the physical body.

Pingala nadi – main nadi on the right side of the body conducting pranashakti, emerging opposite ida, from the right side of mooladhara and intersecting each chakra until it reaches the right side of ajna. Also associated with the mundane realm of existence and conscious experiences. The 'ha' of hatha yoga, indicates the sun or solar force.

Pooja – external worship.

Poojari – worshipper, particularly in a temple.

Poorna shakti – complete manifestation of shakti in the form of Kali, Durga, Laxmi, Saraswati, Parvati; full potential of kundalini.

Prakriti – nature; manifest creation.

Pralaya – dissolution of creation.

Prajna – intuition.

Prana – vital energy force sustaining life and creation, which permeates the whole of creation, existing in both the macro and microcosmos.

Prana prathistha – invoking the cosmic power into a mandala or form of a deity, or body.

Prana shakti – has a wide range of meanings, refers to the cosmic energy force, kundalini and the various manifestations of energy in the body.

Prana vayu – pranic air currents; general name of all the vayus. Also the particular function of vayu in the thoracic region which has an upward movement.

Pranayama – practice of breath and prana control leading to increase in pranic capacity and suspension of breath.

Prasad – blessing given by a deity, guru or saint, usually food.

Prithvi tattwa – earth element.

Purana – legendary narration expounding creation, recreation and genealogies of sages and rulers, altogether eighteen books in number.

Purusha – pure consciousness, male principle.

Purushartha – purpose of the individual consciousness, four in number; kama, artha, dharma, moksha.

Raga – attachment; one of the five afflictions according to Sage Patanjali. According to tantra it is also one of the kanchukas which restricts the capacity or limits the desire and willpower in an individual.

Raja yoga – eightfold path of yoga formulated by Sage Patanjali, known as ashtanga yoga, which begins with mental stability and proceeds to the highest state of samadhi.

Rajas – second quality of maya representing dynamism, movement, and an oscillating state of mind.

Rajoguna – quality of dynamism, oscillation.

Rakini – shakti of dhatu in swadhisthana chakra; one of the amsa roopinis.

Rakshasa – demon, devil, negative force or power.

Rasa tanmatra – subtle principle or essence of taste.

Raudri – consort of Rudra, kinetic principle.

Rishyadi nyasa – a complete ceremony employing exoteric and esoteric symbols, to propel the consciousness through the stages of pratyahara, dharana, dhyana, leading to powers akin to the rishis.

Roopa – form, sight.

Roopa tanmatra – subtle principle or essence of vision, form.

Rudra – name of Shiva in the Rig Veda, denoting a very high state of consciousness.

Sadhaka – spiritual aspirant. A person who is striving on the spiritual path for self-realization, by practising some form of sadhana.

Sadhana – spiritual practice done regularly for attainment of experience and realization of the self, true reality and cosmic consciousness.

Sahasrara chakra – the thousand petalled lotus or chakra manifesting at the top of the head. The highest psychic centre. The threshold between psychic and spiritual realms which contains all the chakras below it.

Sakini – shakti of the dhatu in vishuddhi chakra, one of the amsa roopinis.

Sakshi – aspect of individual consciousness as the silent witness.

Samadhi – final stage of meditation, supraconscious state; unity of object and meditation in the process of meditation.

Samana vayu – pranic air current of the middle region of the body; facilitates assimilation.

Samkhya – the ancient scientific philosophy of India, which classifies the different stages of spiritual experience without any reference to an external power or God.

Samskara – latent impression stored in the subtle body and subconscious mind as an archetype.

Samyama – the threefold process of concentration, meditation and samadhi, which occurs spontaneously through constant practice.

Sankalpa – spiritual resolve, willpower, also a thought.

Sapta dhatu – the seven body minerals of bone, fat, flesh, blood, skin, marrow, and semen/ova.

Saraswati – aspect of poorna shakti; bestower of wisdom, knowledge of fine arts and speech. Creative power of Brahma.

Sattwa – third quality of nature and mind which is steady, pure and unwavering.

Sattwa guna – one of the three qualities of prakriti representing a pure and equilibrated state of nature and mind.

Satya loka – the plane of truth and reality.

Shabda – sound.

Shakti – kinetic principle of consciousness, vital energy force.

Shambhavi – feminine counterpart of Shambhu, representing concentration of mind.

Shambu – literally means, 'born of peace'; a name of Shiva.

Shankhaprakshalana – a technique of dhauti karma in hatha yoga which cleanses the entire alimentary canal by drinking saline water and passing it through the system.

Shanmukhi mudra – particular mudra in which the facial orifices are closed with the fingers.

Shastras – an authoritative treatise on any subject, particularly science and religion.

Shiva – mantra indicating pure consciousness. The supreme reality invoked by the yogis. Name of the deity representing the cosmic state of consciousness.

Shiva tattwa – unconditioned, pure and unified elements of macrocosmos.

Shravan – fifth month of the lunar calendar which takes place from mid-July to mid-August.

Shuddhi – purification.

Siddha – an adept, perfected one; a person who has developed his psychic and pranic capacity of mind and body.

Siddhasana – sitting position in which the left heel presses the perineum, toes of the right foot are placed in between the calf muscle and thigh of the left leg, and heel of the right foot is above the genital organ; a basic meditative pose.

Siddha yoni asana – practised by women, same as siddhasana; the left heel presses the vagina, toes of the right foot are placed between the left calf muscle and thigh.

Siddhi – perfection; activated pranic and psychic capacity and power.

Sparsha tanmatra – subtle principle or essence of touch or feeling.

Sri Aurobindo – world-renowned mahayogi based in Pondicherry, South India, in the early 20th century.

Sthoola sharira – gross body associated with conscious mind.

Srimad Devi Bhagavatam Purana – one of the eighteen puranas which extols the glories of Devi, and contains practices of worship to Shakti.

Sthiti – illumination resulting through concentration which is achieved by refining or purifying the elements.

Sukshma – subtle.

Sukshma sadhana – spiritual practice which directly affects the subtle body and elements.

Sukshma sharira – subtle or astral body, associated with the subconscious mind.

Surya swara – flow of breath in the right nostril only.

Sushupti – unconscious realm and state of mind; deep sleep.

Swapna – dream state, subconscious mind.

Swar – heaven, divine plane of existence.

Tamas – the first quality of nature, inertia.

Tamoguna – quality of inertia, dullness.

Tandava Nritya – the dance of Lord Shiva preceding creation, after which he is named Nataraja.

Tanmatra – subtle or primary essence of gandha (smell), rasa (taste), roopa (sight or form), sparsha (touch), and shabda (sound), from which the tattwas are produced.

Tantra – the oldest science and philosophy of man; the process of expansion of the mind and liberation of energy and consciousness from matter.

Tantric – practitioner of tantra.

Tapo loka – plane of liberated souls.

Tattwa – essential element or principle, 'Thatness'.

Tattwa jnana – knowledge and experience of the elements.

Tattwa Sambara – one of the sixty-four tantras.

Trataka – one of the shatkarma of hatha yoga which entails steadily gazing at an object without blinking.

Triguna – the three gunas, tamas, rajas and sattwa.

Triyambake – the 'three-eyed one' and kinetic aspect of Triyambakam or Shiva.

Turiya – fourth state of consciousness, supraconscious state, the unmanifest state of pure consciousness.

Udana vayu – pranic energy current operating above the throat.

Upanishad – literally means 'to sit close by'. Books of the Veda, traditionally one hundred and eight in number, containing dialogues between guru and disciple on the nature, reality and identity of the individual and cosmic consciousness.

Upaprana – subsidiary prana vayu function.

Upasana – worship, concentration, dharana.

Vairagya – supreme dispassion, non-attachment, state in which one is internally calm and tranquil in the midst of the tumultuous events of the world.

Vamachara – one who practises the doctrines of vama marga tantra.

Vama marga – literally means the 'left path'. Path devised by tantra in which the wife participates in the practices and is considered the guru, includes the panchamakara sadhana of mamsa, matsya, madhya, mudra and maithuna.

Varna – colour.

Vasana – deep-rooted desire.

Vayu – air, see prana vayu.

Vayu tattwa – air element.

Vedas – the oldest written texts revealed to the sages and saints in India, expressing knowledge of the whole universe; four in number, divided into Samhita, Brahmana, Aranyaka and Upanishads.

Vedachara – a path designed by tantra in which the practices are done in accordance with the vedic injunctions.

Vedanta – literally means the culmination of the Veda, or knowledge, i.e. self-realization. The monistic philosophy of Hindus.

Vedantin – one who believes and practices Vedanta.

Vidya tattwa – pure unconditioned and conditioned elements of the microcosmos which create diversity, see maya and kanchukas.

Vijnanamaya kosha – body or sheath made of intuition or higher knowledge.

Vikalpa – imagination, counterthought.

Viparyaya – wrong knowledge, misconception.

Vishuddhi chakra – fifth psychic/pranic energy centre in the middle of the neck corresponding to the cervical plexus.

Vyakta – manifest.

Vyana – pranic air current pervading the whole body.

Yantra – a symbol designed for concentration to unleash the hidden potential energy and consciousness. Abstract

141

form of a mandala, and mantra in perfect mathematical precision represented in the linear dimension.

Yoga – union. A systematic science of the body and mind leading to the union of individual consciousness with the divine principle or cosmic consciousness.

Yoga Sutras – text written by Sage Patanjali, delivering the eightfold path of raja yoga. The systematic path of meditation which culminates in the experience of samadhi.

Yoni – a specially carved stone in which the shiva lingam rests, representing the source of the lingam or atma. See lingam.